Online Interactive Student Book

www.macmillanmh.com

VIEW IT 👁

- Preview weekly concepts and selections

READ IT 📖

- Word-by-Word Reading

LEARN IT 🪐

- Comprehension Questions
- Research and Media Activities

FIND OUT ➤

- Summaries and Glossary in other Languages

LOG ON ▶ **Online Activities**
www.macmillanmh.com

- **Interactive activities** and **animated lessons** for guided instruction and practice

IWB Interactive White Board Ready!

Treasures

A Reading/Language Arts Program

Mc Graw Hill **Macmillan/McGraw-Hill**

Contributors

Time Magazine, Accelerated Reader

learning through listening

Students with print disabilities may be eligible to obtain an accessible, audio version of the pupil edition of this textbook. Please call Recording for the Blind & Dyslexic at 1-800-221-4792 for complete information.

B

The *McGraw·Hill* Companies

Macmillan/McGraw-Hill

Published by Macmillan/McGraw-Hill, of McGraw-Hill Education, a division of The McGraw-Hill Companies, Inc., Two Penn Plaza, New York, New York 10121.

Printed in the United States of America

ISBN: 978-0-02-201731-6
MHID: 0-02-201731-3

2 3 4 5 6 7 8 9 DOW 13 12 11 10

Treasures

A Reading/Language Arts Program

Program Authors

Diane August
Donald R. Bear
Janice A. Dole
Jana Echevarria
Douglas Fisher
David Francis
Vicki Gibson
Jan E. Hasbrouck
Scott G. Paris
Timothy Shanahan
Josefina V. Tinajero

 Macmillan/McGraw-Hill

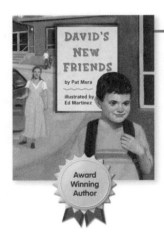

Social Studies

Community Heroes

Unit 3

Creative Expression
Let's Create

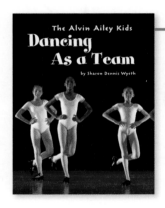

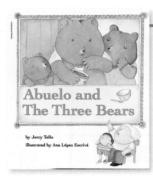

The **Big** Question

Think about what makes a good friend.

LOG ON ▶ VIEW IT

Theme Video
Friends and Family
www.macmillanmh.com

What are the qualities of a good friend?

Classmates, family members, neighbors, and pets can be friends. Friends often live nearby, but sometimes friends live far away. Some friends like the same things we do.

Our friends can also be very different from us. Friends can teach us new things, play games with us, help us, and support us when we try new things. We want to spend our time with good friends.

Learning about different kinds of friends helps us learn what we can do to be better friends.

Research Activities

During this unit you will gather information. As a class we will create a list of kinds of friends and write open-ended questions. Choose a friend. Research and create a biography about the friend.

Keep Track of Ideas

As you read, keep track of all you are learning about different friends. Use the **Shutter Study Foldable** to record what you learn. Across the top, write the unit theme Friends and Family. Under each shutter, write facts about friends that you learn each week.

Teamwork and Rules

When talking about Friends and Family with the class, it is important to agree on and follow rules.

- Listen to others.
- Raise your hand to speak.
- Ask questions and make comments when called on.

Discuss with the class other rules that are important to follow.

Digital Learning

LOG ON ▶ FIND OUT www.macmillanmh.com

StudentWorks Plus
Interactive Student Book

- **Research Roadmap**
  Follow a step-by-step guide to complete your research project.

Online Resources

- Topic Finder and Other Research Tools
- Videos and Virtual Field Trips
- Photos and Drawings for Presentations
- Related Articles and Web Resources
- Web Site Links

People and Places

Helen Keller and Anne Sullivan

Helen Keller and Anne Sullivan met in 1887. Anne was Helen Keller's teacher. She taught Helen, who was both blind and deaf, how to read and write.

Friends at School

Talk About It

What do you do with friends at school? How do you get to know new students?

LOG ON ▶ VIEW IT

Oral Language Activities
School Friends
www.macmillanmh.com

Vocabulary

groan
excited
whisper
carefully
different

✔ Dictionary

When words are in alphabetical order, they are listed in ABC order.

The following words are in alphabetical order:

carefully
different
excited

School Is Starting!

by Josh Santos

Tom, Matt, and Lea played in the park. "Today is the last day of summer," said Tom. "Tomorrow is the first day of school!"

"I always **groan** when summer ends," Matt said. He made a noise to show he was upset.

"We can't play all day when school starts," said Lea. "But I am still **excited**. I feel very happy about school this year. It's going to be fun!"

"I'm not so sure," Matt said.

"Really?" Lea asked Matt.

"I meant to **whisper** that," said Matt. "I wanted to say it softly. I did not want you to hear that I am scared."

Tom **carefully** climbed up the slide. He went up slowly so he would not fall. He slid down and smiled at Matt.

"It's okay, Matt," Tom said. "I am nervous, too. Second grade will be **different**. Nothing will be the same. But one thing is for sure. We will always be friends!"

Reread for **Comprehension**

Analyze Story Structure

Character and Setting

Thinking about a story's structure, or the way it is organized, can help you understand more about the **characters** and the **setting**. Reread the story and use the chart to help you understand the people in the story and where it takes place.

Character	Setting

LOG ON ▶ LEARN IT Comprehension
www.macmillanmh.com

9

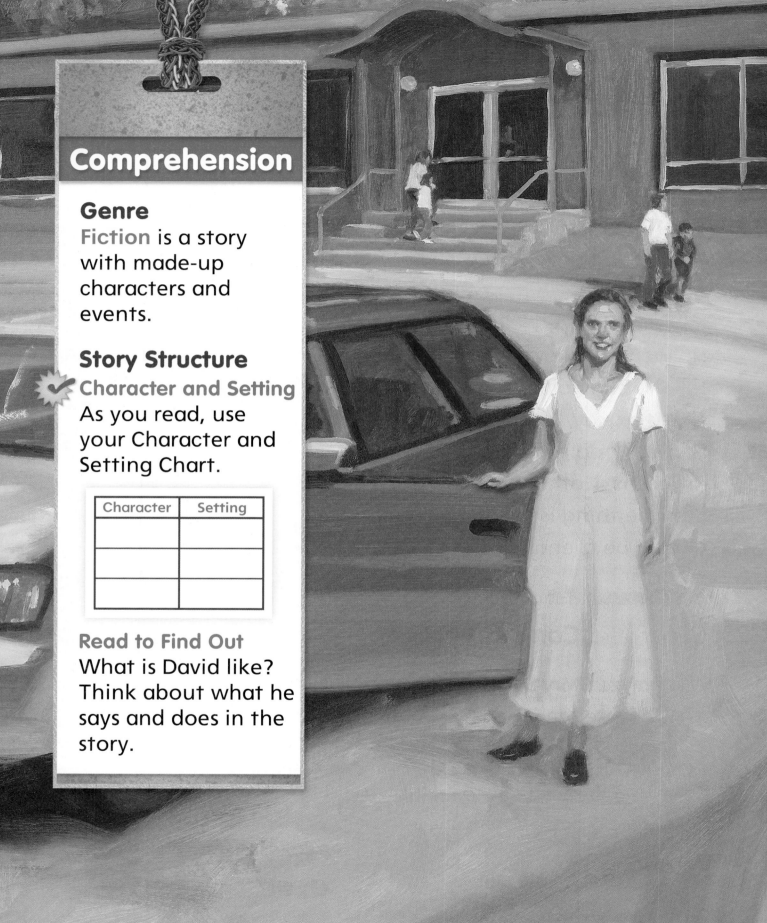

Comprehension

Genre
Fiction is a story with made-up characters and events.

Story Structure
Character and Setting
As you read, use your Character and Setting Chart.

Character	Setting

Read to Find Out
What is David like? Think about what he says and does in the story.

DAVID'S NEW FRIENDS

by Pat Mora

illustrated by
Ed Martinez

11

"Tomorrow is the first day of school, David," Mom says. "Are you glad?"

"I guess."

My mom is a teacher. She really likes school. I like school, too, but the first day is **different**. Everything is new.

My sister Linda asks me to read to her. She hands me a book about lizards.

"Ugh," I **groan**. "Let's read about tigers. I don't like creepy lizards."

I read to my sister, but I think about school, too. Will I like my teacher? Will I meet new friends?

The next morning, Grandma hands me my backpack. "You are a big boy now," she says. "You're in second grade!"

I try to act big. Then I give her a hug. Mom drives me to school.

"Aren't you **excited**, David? You're going to see your school friends."

"Yes," I answer. But also I hope I'll meet some new ones, too.

My new classroom is full of neat stuff. Maybe this year *will* be fun.

I see Ron and Josie near the fish tank. I want to tell them about my trip to the zoo. Then I see the lizard. Ugh! I sit on the other side of the room.

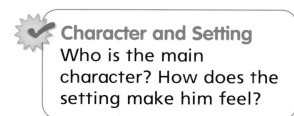

Character and Setting
Who is the main character? How does the setting make him feel?

Our teacher is standing by the chalkboard.
"Good morning, girls and boys," he says. "I'm your
new teacher, Mr. Roy." He gives the class a big grin.
Then he looks around. "Where's the chalk?"
he asks.

I get up and hand him some chalk.

Mr. Roy smiles. "Thanks, David."

"Okay," Mr. Roy says. "Let's begin!" He looks around. "Now, where are my glasses?"

I point to his head.

"What are you doing up there?" he asks his glasses. Everyone laughs. Mr. Roy gives me a wink.

I like this teacher.

We finish math at 10:00. Then it's snack time. Everyone gets juice to drink. Mr. Roy spills some on his shoes. I give him my napkin.

Mr. Roy says to me, "Oh no, David! These are my slippers. I was so excited this morning, I forgot to put on my shoes!" We laugh together.

"Okay, girls and boys," says Mr. Roy. "It's time to meet a friend of mine." He picks up the lizard.

"Oh no!" I say to myself. "Not the lizard!"

"His name is Slim," says Mr. Roy. "He's thin like me."

The class giggles.

Mr. Roy says, "I hold him **carefully** so I don't hurt him."

> ✔ **Character and Setting**
> How do you think the main character feels about Slim? Use story details.

Just then, Slim slips out of Mr. Roy's hand.

Everyone starts yelling.

Slim is as fast as a whip.

He runs under desks.

He runs over feet.

He runs around the trashcan.

Then he runs right at me!

"Catch him, David!" yells Mr. Roy.

I take a deep breath and drop to my knees.

All the kids stay very still. Everyone is watching me.

"Here, Slim," I **whisper**. "I won't hurt you."
I move very slowly. I get closer and closer.
I look into Slim's bright eyes, and then—
I GRAB HIM!

23

I feel Slim wiggle in my hands. I can tell
that he's afraid.

"Don't worry, Slim," I say quietly. "We
won't hurt you."

I put Slim back in the tank. He runs under
a twig and then peeks out. He winks at me!

Mr. Roy says, "I think he likes you, David."

I think I like him, too.

At the end of the day, Mr. Roy stops me at the door. "Thanks for your help today, my friend," he says smiling.

Grandma and Linda are waiting for me after school.

"Wow!" I say. "I have a great new teacher. He's my friend. And guess what?"

"What?" asks Linda.

"I have another friend, too. His name is Slim. He's a lizard!"

MEET NEW FRIENDS PAT AND ED

Author **PAT MORA** says many of the ideas for her books come from the things she likes best. Some things she likes are families and folk tales. Pat is special because she can speak and write in both English and Spanish!

When artist **ED MARTINEZ** was in college, he saw a TV show about children's book illustrators. He decided then that he wanted to illustrate books, too.

Other books written by Pat Mora

by **Pat Mora** • illustrated by **Cecily Lang**

LOG ON ▶ FIND OUT

Author Pat Mora
Illustrator Ed Martinez
www.macmillanmh.com

✔ Author's Purpose

Pat Mora writes about a boy starting second grade. Think about your first day of second grade. Write about that day.

✔ Comprehension Check

Retell the Story

Use the Retelling Cards to retell the story.

Retelling Cards

Think and Compare

Character	Setting

1. What grade will David start when school begins? **Facts**

2. Reread pages 12–15. How does David feel before he goes to school? Use the text to explain how you know. **Character**

3. Use details from the story to explain how the setting changes David's feelings about school. **Setting**

4. How is David different after his first day of school? What might the author want readers to learn from what happened to David? **Character**

5. Read "School Is Starting" on pages 8–9. How is Matt like David? Tell how you know. **Reading/Writing Across Texts**

27

Science

Genre
Expository text gives information about real people, things, or events.

✔ **Text Feature**
Photos and Captions give more information about a topic. Captions tell about the photos.

Content Vocabulary
habitat

data

record

Field Trip to an Aquarium

Welcome back to school! It's time for a learning adventure. Have you ever seen a shark swim? Have you seen a sea horse up close? You don't have to dive under the sea to do this. You can watch ocean animals in an aquarium.

Sharks need room to swim. Some aquariums are two times larger than swimming pools.

An aquarium is a model of an ocean **habitat**. It has everything that ocean animals need to live and grow. In an aquarium, sea animals swim in big glass tanks filled with salt water. There are waves and caves.

Sea animals need food, light, and air. In an aquarium, workers feed the animals. Lamps light the tanks. Filters clean the water. Heaters warm it. Air bubbles flow into the tanks so the animals can breathe.

▲
The sun warms the ocean and gives it light. In an aquarium, lamps light the water.

Scientists study aquarium animals. They see how life in an aquarium changes. There may be changes in eating habits. Scientists ask questions. How do sea animals act in summer? Does this change in winter? Scientists gather **data**, or information. They **record** what they find.

Maybe one day your class will have an aquarium.

▲ Scientists study sea animals. Some scientists treat sick animals.

▼ These children do what scientists do. They take care of the aquarium and observe.

The tank may not be big, but it can be a model of an ocean habitat. You can study fish and plants that live under water. You can see an underwater world at work!

Coral look like rock, but they ▶ are tiny sea animals. Millions of them can form a reef.

Connect and Compare

1. What is coral? Where did you find the information to answer the question? **Photos and Captions**

2. Think about the story *David's New Friends.* What might David and the class think about having an aquarium of fish in the room? **Reading/Writing Across Texts**

 Science Activity

Research two different kinds of coral. Make a chart listing how they are the same and how they are different.

LOG ON ▶ FIND OUT **Science** Aquariums www.macmillanmh.com

Writing

✓ **Topic Sentence**

A **topic sentence** tells the reader what the writing is about.

Reading and Writing Connection

This is *my* topic sentence.

Here I tell what this paragraph is about.

Ready for School!
by Eileen S.

Today was the first day of school. I was so excited I woke up very early. I decided to wear *my* red pants and *my* lucky striped socks. Then I sat down to eat breakfast.

The next thing I knew, *my* mom was shaking me. I had wet hair. My face was sticky. What happened? I had fallen asleep in *my* cereal bowl!

Your Writing Prompt

The first day of school is exciting.

Think about what you did on your first day of school. Did you see old friends or make new ones?

Write about it. Include a strong topic sentence. Be sure to include a beginning, middle, and end.

Writer's Checklist

✓ My writing is a personal account of my first day at school this year.

✓ I include a strong topic sentence that tells what my writing is about.

✓ I include details that give more information about the topic.

✓ All my sentences are complete and begin with a capital letter.

Pet Friends

Talk About It

Why are pets good friends?

LOG ON ▶ **VIEW IT**

Oral Language Activities
Pet Friends
www.macmillanmh.com

35

Making Muffins and a Friend

by Vanessa Gutierrez

"Don't forget," Ms. Kim said. "Tomorrow you must bring in something to **share** with the class. Please bring something that all of us can look at. It could be a book that you **enjoyed**. You can tell us why you liked it so much."

Pam's friends had **wonderful** ideas. Pam did not have any great ideas like theirs. After the bell rang, the class began **thinning** out. The students left the classroom one by one. Soon only Pam and Marco were left. Pam asked Marco about his idea.

"I think I might cook," he said. "Let's make something together!"

They decided to make muffins. Pam was **delighted**. She was very happy to have an idea at last.

Making muffins was not easy. The mix was too thick. They had to add a lot of milk to fix it. The muffins were not perfect, but Pam and Marco did not care. Being together was fun. The best thing to share was the **company** of a new friend!

Reread for **Comprehension**

Story Structure

 Plot

Thinking about a story's structure, or the way it is organized, can help you understand the **plot**. The plot is what happens at the beginning, middle, and end of a story.

Reread the story and use the Story Map to describe the plot.

| Beginning |
| Middle |
| End |

LOG ON ▶ LEARN IT Comprehension
www.macmillanmh.com

Comprehension

Genre
Fiction is a story with made-up characters and events.

Story Structure
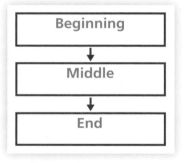
Plot
As you read, use your Story Map.

Beginning
↓
Middle
↓
End

Read to Find Out
What happens to Mr. Putter in the beginning, middle, and end of this story?

38

Mr. Putter & Tabby Pour the Tea

by Cynthia Rylant
illustrated by Arthur Howard

Award Winning Author

40

Chapter
1

Mr. Putter

Before he got his fine cat, Tabby,
Mr. Putter lived all alone.

In the mornings he had no one
to **share** his English muffins.
In the afternoons he had no one
to share his tea.

And in the evenings
there was no one
Mr. Putter could
tell his stories to.
And he had the
most **wonderful**
stories to tell.

All day long as Mr. Putter
clipped his roses
and fed his tulips
and watered his trees,
Mr. Putter wished for
some **company**.

He had warm muffins to eat.

He had good tea to pour.

And he had wonderful stories to tell.

Mr. Putter was tired of living alone.

Mr. Putter wanted a cat.

Plot
Use story details to describe the story's plot so far. What does Mr. Putter want? Why?

Chapter

Tabby

Mr. Putter went to the pet store.
"Do you have any cats?" he asked the
pet store lady.
"We have fourteen," she said.
Mr. Putter was **delighted.**
But when he looked into the cage,
he was not.

"These are kittens," he said.
"I was hoping for a cat."
"Oh, no one wants cats, sir,"
said the pet store lady.
"They are not cute.
They are not peppy."

Mr. Putter himself had not
been cute and peppy for a
very long time.
He said, "I want a cat."
"Then go to the shelter, sir,"
said the pet store lady.
"You are sure to find a cat."

Mr. Putter went to the shelter.
"Have you any cats?"
he asked the shelter man.
"We have a fat gray one,
a thin black one,
and an old yellow one," said the man.
"Did you say old?" asked Mr. Putter.

The shelter man brought Mr. Putter
the old yellow cat.
Its bones creaked,
its fur was **thinning**,
and it seemed a little deaf.
Mr. Putter creaked,
his hair was thinning,
and he was a little deaf, too.

So he took the old yellow cat home.
He named her Tabby.
And that is how their life began.

Chapter 3
Mr. Putter and Tabby

In the mornings
Mr. Putter and Tabby liked to share
an English muffin.
Mr. Putter ate his with jam.
Tabby ate hers with cream cheese.

In the afternoons
Mr. Putter and Tabby
liked to share tea.
Mr. Putter took his with sugar.
Tabby took hers with cream.

And in the evenings
they sat by the window,
and Mr. Putter told stories.
He told the most wonderful stories.
Each story made Tabby purr.

On summer days they warmed their
old bones together in the sun.
On fall days they took
long walks through the trees.
And on winter days they turned
the opera up *very* loud.

Mr. Putter could not remember
life without Tabby.
Tabby could not remember
life without Mr. Putter.
They lived among their
tulips and trees.

They ate their muffins.

They poured their tea.

They turned up the opera,
and **enjoyed** the most
perfect company of all—
each other.

Plot
Think about the story's plot.
What does Mr. Putter do in
each chapter of this story? Use
illustrations and story details.

Cat "Mews" From Cynthia and Arthur

Cynthia Rylant has written many books. When she gets an idea, she says, "I sit down with pen and paper, and soon I've got a story going!" She has two cats named Boris and Blossom. Boris gets into trouble, but "Blossom is perfect," Cynthia says. Which cat do you think is like Tabby?

Arthur Howard illustrates all of the Mr. Putter and Tabby books. When Arthur started the series, he drew Mr. Putter to look like his father. He based Tabby on his mother's cat, Red.

Other books written by Cynthia Rylant

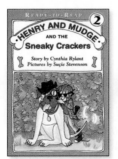

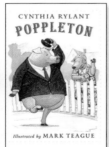

LOG ON ▶ FIND OUT

Author Cynthia Rylant
Illustrator Arthur Howard
www.macmillanmh.com

✔ Author's Purpose

Cynthia Rylant and Arthur Howard use people and animals they know to help them create stories. Write about a person or an animal that you know.

✔ Comprehension Check

Retell the Story

Use the Retelling Cards to retell the story.

Retelling Cards

Think and Compare

1. Where does Mr. Putter live? **Facts**

2. Reread pages 56–58. How does Mr. Putter's life change after he gets some **company**? **Story Structure: Plot**

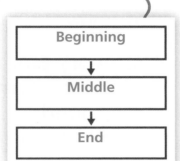

3. What can you conclude about Mr. Putter and Tabby? Use details from the story that support your answer. **Character**

4. Why does the author describe Mr. Putter and Tabby in the same way? **Character**

5. Read "Making Muffins and a Friend" on pages 36–37. How are Pam and Marco like Mr. Putter and Tabby? **Reading/Writing Across Texts**

Genre
A **Rhyming Poem** has lines that end with the same rhyming sounds.

✔ Literary Elements
Rhythmic Patterns are sounds and words that repeat to give a song or poem a certain rhythm.

Words that **Rhyme** begin with different sounds but end with the same sound.

Rhyme, rhythm, and repetition help create images in poetry.

Cat Kisses

by Bobbi Katz

Sandpaper kisses
on a cheek or a chin
that is the way
for a day to begin!
Sandpaper kisses
a cuddle, a purr.
I have an alarm clock
that's covered with fur.

⭐ **Connect and Compare**

1. What are some pairs of words that rhyme in this poem? **Rhyme**

2. Think about Mr. Putter and Tabby. Do you think the person in this poem feels the same way about her cat that Mr. Putter does about Tabby? Explain why or why not. **Reading/Writing Across Texts**

LOG ON ▶ FIND OUT Poetry
www.macmillanmh.com

Reading and Writing Connection

Writing

✔ Vary Sentences

Good writers vary sentence types to make their writing more interesting.

My Funny Friend
by Benny B.

The topic sentence is a statement.

I used an exclamation to show excitement.

My best friend, Jenny, lives next door to me. We have been friends a long time. Jenny has freckles and long, red hair. She also wears glasses like I do! Jenny likes to tell jokes and riddles. When I want to laugh, I go visit my funny friend.

Your Writing Prompt

A friend is a person or pet you
know well and like.

Think about a person
or pet who is your friend.

Now write a
paragraph that tells
about your friend.

Writer's Checklist

☑   I used **different types of sentences**
to tell about a friend whom I know well
and like.

☑   I wrote a clear topic sentence.

☑   I wrote details that tell about
my friend.

☑   My spelling is correct. I used capital
letters in the right places.

Talk About It

Why can family members also be friends? What do families do together?

LOG ON ▶ VIEW IT

Oral Language Activities
Family Friends
www.macmillanmh.com

Family
Friends

Vocabulary

- machines
- harvest
- regrow
- irrigate
- crops

A Nutty State

These orchards produce millions of pounds of pecans for the state of Texas.

Pecan trees grow along the banks of nearly every river in Texas. No wonder the pecan tree is the state tree of Texas! About 60 million pounds of pecans come from Texas every year.

Native Americans were the first people to know about pecans. It was an important part of their diet.

Long ago people had to climb the tall trees to pick pecans. Or they threw sticks into the trees to make the nuts fall. Today farmers use **machines** to **harvest** pecans. These machines shake the trees to make the pecans fall. Another machine picks up the nuts. Thanks to pecan farmers, everyone can taste these Texas treats.

Moving Water

Farmers can't grow or **regrow** food crops without water. In the Southwest the weather is hot and dry. So farmers often must **irrigate** their land. That means they bring water from one place to another. Long ago Texas farmers made long ditches called canals. The canals carried river water to farms. In the Rio Grande Valley, water from the river helped farmers grow **crops** such as oranges.

Some Texas farmland sits on an underground sea of water. In the past farmers sank pipes into the earth and built windmills. Today electric pumps bring up water. Now Texas farmers can grow many kinds of crops.

Water is brought up from the ground by electric pumps to the growing crops.

69

FAMILY FARM
Then and Now

How did farming begin in the United States?

Thousands of years before people from Europe and Africa arrived in North America, Native Americans were successful farmers. They grew beans, corn, squash, and cotton. In the dry Southwest, Native Americans dug canals to bring water from rivers to their **crops**. Bringing water to crops is called irrigation.

Animals such as horses and oxen helped farmers plow the land and plant crops.

70

When Europeans arrived, they learned about farming from the Native Americans. They learned to grow and **regrow** the crops they needed for food.

Native American and European farmers had very different ideas about owning land. Most Native American groups believed that the land belonged to everyone. Land was to be used by any family that was willing to work on it. The Europeans believed that one person or family should own the land. The owner could keep the land or sell it. This difference often caused trouble between the Native Americans and settlers.

Native Americans and new settlers share the land.

71

New Settlers

As more and more settlers arrived, they moved further west to get land of their own. They crossed the Mississippi River and kept going. The government helped them claim large pieces of land. They built houses, cleared the land, and began farming.

Farmland was passed down from family to family. Children whose parents were farmers usually grew up to become farmers. Family members did most of the work themselves. They earned money by selling their crops. They also sold milk and meat from the farm animals they raised.

Families worked together to farm the land and sell their crops.

Machines help today's farmers clear fields, plant seeds, and harvest crops.

Today there are fewer family farms. The family farms that remain are bigger. Modern ways of farming make it easier to grow more crops. Electric pumps **irrigate** huge fields. **Machines** help farmers clear fields, plant seeds, and **harvest** crops.

Many farms today are owned by companies. The people who work on these farms are employees of the company.

Every year the number of family farms gets smaller. Children move away. Farmland is sold. Family farming may become a thing of the past, but it will always be an important part of American history.

✔ Think and Compare

1. Who were the first successful farmers?

2. Why is farming land as important today as it was in the past?

3. What is the main idea of this selection?

4. Based on "A Nutty State" and "Family Farm," how have machines changed farming?

A Farmer's Helping Hand

1 Farmers have a tough job. They must plant seeds and irrigate land to grow and regrow crops season after season. Then they harvest, or gather, the crops. Machines make those jobs easier. Tractors help farmers plow a field. Before tractors, farmers used horses or mules to plow the ground. Another machine drops seeds into the ground. In the past, farmers walked along the fields and dropped seeds by hand.

2 Farm hands took days to harvest crops. Today's machines now do all the work. A combine can cut, gather, and clean crops. Today's machines save farmers time and money. They help farmers produce more food for our tables.

DIRECTIONS
Decide which is the best answer to each question.

1 What helped farmers plow before tractors?

  A Combines

  B Machines

  C Seeds or crops

  D Horses or mules

2 Before machines, farmers used to —

  A grow more crops

  B do work by hand

  C have an easier job

  D eat more vegetables

3 The author most likely wrote this article to —

  A tell how machines help farmers

  B explain how to plant crops

  C tell why farms are important

  D show how to become a farmer

4 What is the best summary of the article?

  A Machines make farming easier than in the past. They cut, gather, and clean crops.

  B Farmers have tough jobs. They drive tractors and plow fields every summer.

  C Machines save farmers time and money. They can plant seeds.

  D Combines cut, gather, and clean crops. They produce food for the table.

Write to a Prompt

Pablo wrote about the way his grandmother taught him to make lemonade.

I made sure that my ideas are clear and organized.

Old-Fashioned Fun

I spend every Saturday afternoon with my grandmother. She teaches me how to do all sorts of new things. Last Saturday, Grandma showed me how to make old-fashioned lemonade. First, Grandma cut some lemons in half. Next, she showed me how to squeeze out all the juice. Then we added water and a little sugar to the lemon juice. Last, I stirred everything together in a pitcher. I put some ice in two glasses and Grandma poured the lemonade. I took a sip and it was delicious!

Writing Prompt

Respond in writing to the prompt below. Review the hints below before and after you write.

Write about something you learned from a friend.

Writing Hints

- ☑ Remember to write about something you learned from a friend.

- ☑ Plan your writing by organizing your ideas.

- ☑ Include important details to support your ideas.

- ☑ Check that each sentence you write helps the reader understand your writing.

- ☑ Use correct spelling, capitalization, punctuation, grammar, and sentences.

- ☑ Review and edit your writing.

Special Friends

Talk About It

Every person is different. What makes your friend special?

LOG ON ▶ **VIEW IT**

Oral Language Activities
Special Friends
www.macmillanmh.com

Vocabulary

cultures
deaf
signing
relatives
celebrate

✔ Dictionary

Using resources is one way to **clarify** information in a text. You can use a dictionary or other reference books to look up new meanings for words you know.

signing: showing words and letters with your hands and fingers. *verb*

A Special Camp

by Kate Jones

Camp Taloali (ta-loe-AL-ee) in Oregon is a special place. The campers and counselors come from many backgrounds and **cultures**. Almost everyone at Taloali is **deaf**, which means they cannot hear.

If campers cannot hear, how do they know what someone is saying to them? One way is through sign language. Sign language is a way that people can talk to one another without speaking. **Signing** is a way to show words and letters with your hands and fingers. It is like a code.

Some **relatives** of deaf children started Camp Taloali. They wanted the deaf people in their family to have a camp like hearing children have.

At the end of each summer, the campers **celebrate** with a big party. They remember all the fun times they had together. Then they sign good-bye to their new friends.

Reread for **Comprehension**

Summarize

Main Idea and Details One way to summarize is to identify the main idea, or the most important idea in an article. Facts and details from the text give more information about the main idea. Reread the article and use the chart to help you understand the main idea and details.

Detail	Detail	Detail

Main Idea

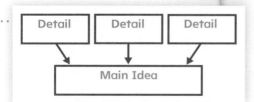

LOG ON ▶ LEARN IT Comprehension
www.macmillanmh.com

81

Comprehension

Genre

Expository A photo essay uses mostly photographs to give information about a topic.

Summarize

✔ **Main Idea and Details**
As you read, use your Main Idea and Details Web.

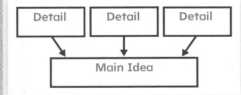

Read to Find Out
Who is Rosina? Tell what details you find out about her.

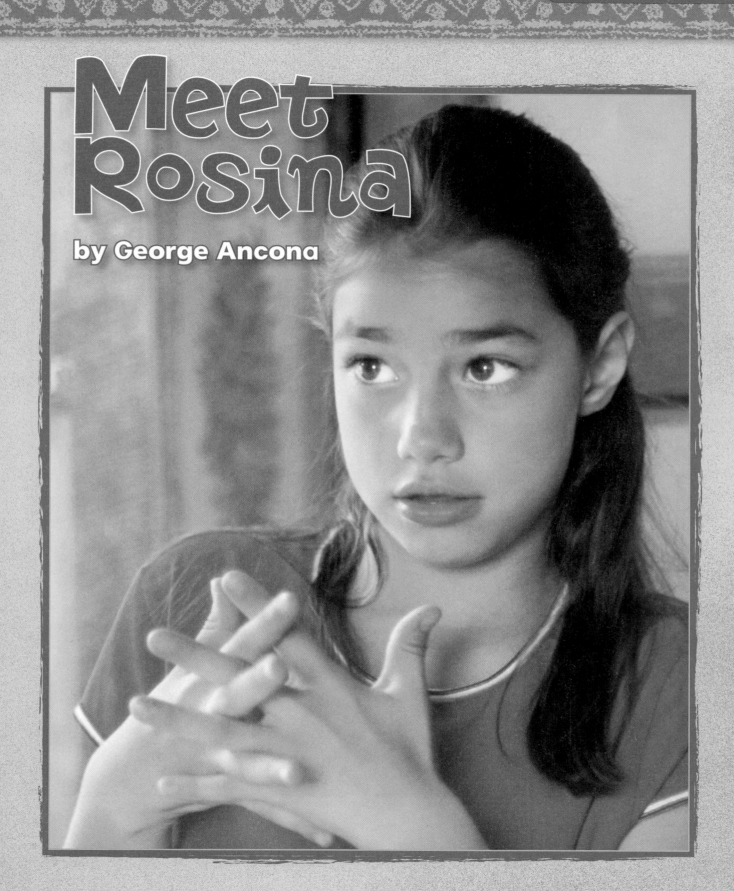

Meet Rosina

by George Ancona

Hi!   I'm

    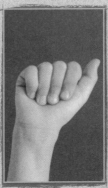

R   o   s   i   n   a

I am **deaf**, so I talk with my hands.

I go to the New Mexico School for the Deaf. All of our teachers teach with American Sign Language. We call this **signing**.

We study math, writing, reading, and art. We also play sports. It's the same as in other schools.

✔️ **Main Idea and Details**
Use facts and details from the selection to describe Rosina's school.

My brother Emilio also goes to my school. After lunch, we play basketball during recess.

My mom and aunt are deaf, too. They work at the school. Mom is a teacher's helper.

Mom came from Mexico when she was little. She had to learn American Sign Language so that she could learn English. That's because each country has its own way of signing.

Aunt Carla's job is to help students and teachers learn about different **cultures**. She also takes care of the school museum.

In the museum there are pictures of our **relatives** who went to the school. Aunt Carla often tells me fun stories about when my parents were younger. She told me that my parents met each other at a high school dance.

Sometimes we go to the school library.
Our librarian, Hedy, signs stories from the
books in the library.

Hedy is very good at telling stories. She makes us feel as if we're in the story. The story can make us feel sad, scared, worried, or happy.

I love going to art class. I like to paint using watercolors. Here I am painting a picture of myself!

When we were in second grade, our class made up a story. It was about a deaf dad who woke up one day with four arms. We wrote it and did all the drawings. Then we made it into a book called *Too Many Hands*.

Our book was published! Today we had a book signing. We wrote our names in the books that people bought.

I like sports. This year I am playing rugby. The way we play is to tag the person carrying the ball. Then he or she throws it to another player on the team. By running fast we can get away and cross the goal line.

Our team played other schools at the end of the year. We beat all the other teams and won a big trophy.

Then we wanted to **celebrate**. We splashed our coach with cold water. Some of us got wet, too. We were just joking, so no one got mad.

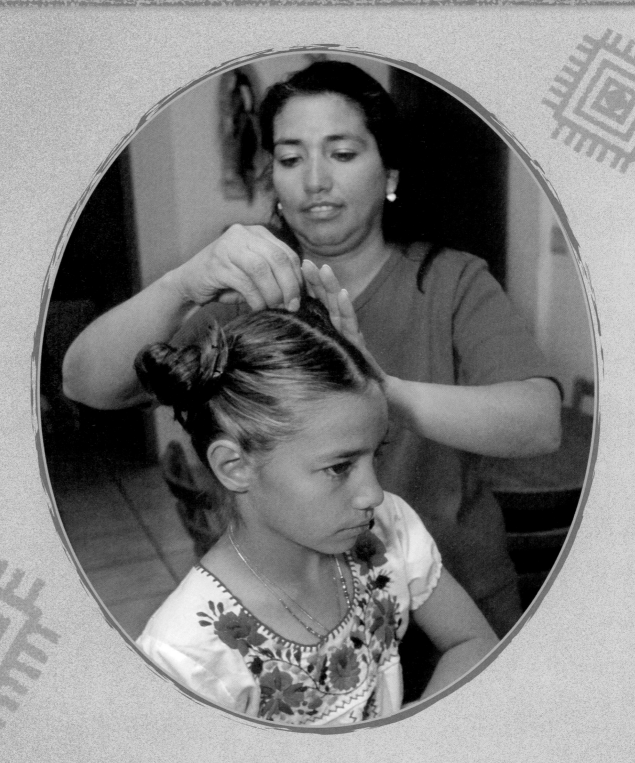

After school I shower and change clothes for dinner. Mom likes to fix my hair. She puts it up in a bun like her mother did.

At home we all help Mom cook Mexican meals. While I chop the lettuce, Emilio cuts up cheese. Dad makes the guacamole. Then I fry the tacos.

After dinner, Dad and I play a game of chess. Emilio roots for me. He's hoping that I win, but Dad wins anyway.

✔ **Main Idea and Details**
Think about Rosina's day. What are three details you find interesting? Why?

Mom, Dad, Emilio, and me. That's my family—but there are many more, too.

We are a big family. I have lots of uncles, aunts, cousins, grandpas, and grandmas. My father's family was among the first Spanish people that came to New Mexico. That was 500 years ago.

Most of my mom's family is deaf. My whole family uses sign language to talk to each other.

This is how we sign "goodbye."

Taking Photos and Making Smiles with George Ancona

George Ancona wrote the words and took the photographs for this selection. He learned how to take photographs from his father when he was growing up. His father developed pictures in their bathroom!

Today George likes to photograph people in their everyday lives. Meeting all kinds of people is what he enjoys the most. Before George wrote this book, he already knew some sign language. In this picture, he is signing, "I love you!"

Other books written by George Ancona

Author George Ancona
www.macmillanmh.com

✔ Author's Purpose

George Ancona shows how Rosina spends a day. Write a journal entry about what you did yesterday.

✔ Comprehension Check

Retell the Selection

Use the Retelling Cards to retell the selection using the vocabulary words *deaf*, *signing* and *relatives*.

Retelling Cards

Think and Compare

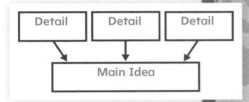

Detail	Detail	Detail

Main Idea

1. Where does Rosina go to school? **Details**

2. What does Rosina do when she is at school? Use details from the text to support your answer. **Details**

3. What do all the important details in the selection tell about Rosina? **Main Idea and Details**

4. Why does the author write about Rosina's day? **Author's Purpose**

5. Read "A Special Camp" on pages 80–81. Do you think Rosina would like to go to Camp Taloali? Explain. **Reading/Writing Across Texts**

103

Genre
A **Rhyming Poem** has lines that end with the same rhyming sounds.

Words that Rhyme begin with different sounds but end with the same sound.

YOU-TÚ

by Charlotte Pomerantz

You are you.	Tú eres tú.
Not me,	No yo,
But you.	Pero tú.
Look in the mirror	Mira al espejo
Peek-a-boo	Peek-a-boo
The face that you see	La cara que miras
Isn't me—	No soy yo—
It's you.	Eres tú.

Connect and Compare

1. Where are the rhyming words in this poem? **Rhyme**

2. Think about the poem and *Meet Rosina*. How do you think Rosina would feel about this poem? Explain why. **Reading/Writing Across Texts**

LOG ON ▶ FIND OUT **Poetry** Rhyming Poems
www.macmillanmh.com

Reading and Writing Connection

✔ **Important Details**

Good writing includes **important details**. When you write, think about what details the reader needs to know.

These first two details tell Josie about who I am.

This detail tells about what I like to do.

September 19, 2–––

Dear Josie,

→ My name is Wendy. I am seven years old. I am in second grade and live in Texas. The thing I like to do best is ride → my bike with my friends. We go bike riding in the park near my house. Do you like to bike ride?

Write back soon. Tell me all about you!

Sincerely,
Wendy

Your Writing Prompt

Everyone has an activity that he or she likes to do with a friend.

Think about what you like to do.

Write a friendly letter to a new friend telling about what you like to do.

Writer's Checklist

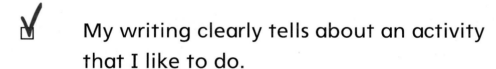

✓ My writing clearly tells about an activity that I like to do.

✓ I present the main idea of what I like to do, and then I support it with detailed information.

☑ I include **important details** that give information about me and what I like.

✓ Each sentence has a subject and a predicate. Each sentence is complete and ends with the correct punctuation.

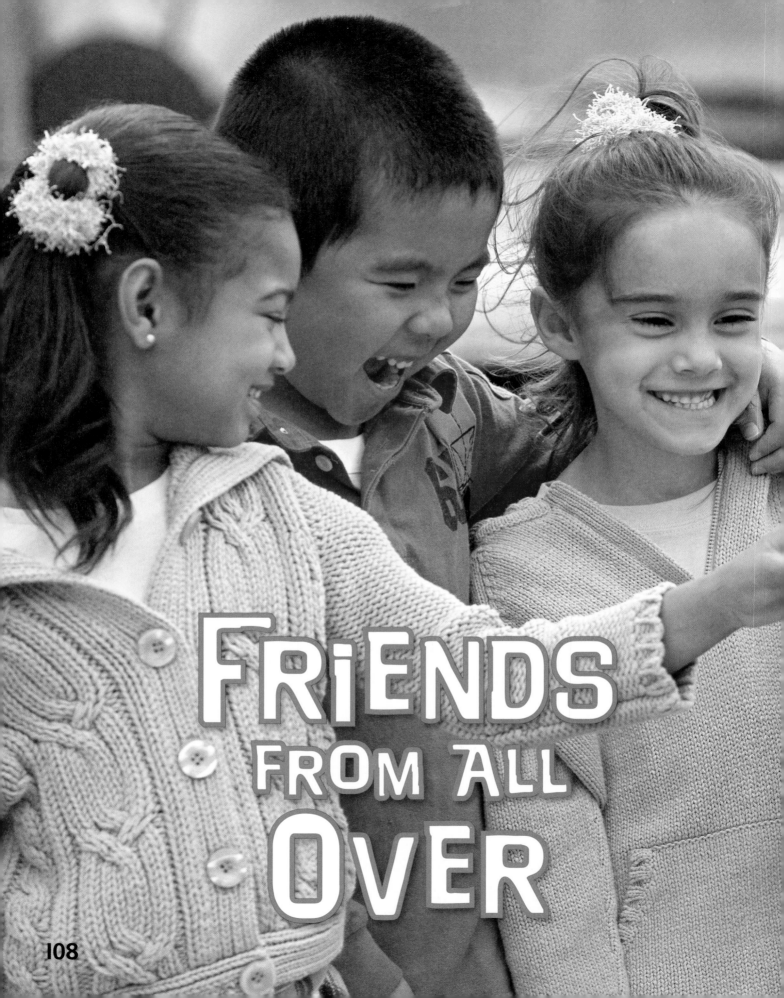

FRiENDS FROM ALL OVER

Talk About It

Think about your friends from different places. What makes these friendships special?

LOG ON ▶ VIEW IT

Oral Language Activities
Friendship
www.macmillanmh.com

My New HOME

by Miguel Vasquez

May 3

We are here in America at last. The airplane trip from Argentina was long. It was hard to be **patient**. I could hardly wait to get here.

I met a boy named Pat on the plane. We spoke both English and Spanish. I told him I had **practiced** my English for years in school. Of all my school subjects, English is my **favorite**. I like it the best.

May 10

Two days ago we got to our new home. When we went inside I **wrinkled** my nose. I smelled something different. Our neighbor was cooking spicy food.

Now my family is unpacking and getting **settled**. My dad got me a cute kitten named Carla. When I miss Argentina, I **cuddle** her and hold her close. Then I feel better.

Reread for **Comprehension**

Summarize

✦ **Make and Confirm Predictions**
Summarizing can help you make predictions, or guesses, about what happens in a story. You can use ideas, pictures, titles, or key words to help make predictions. Reread the first journal entry and use the chart to make and confirm predictions about what happens in the next entry.

What I Predict	What Happens

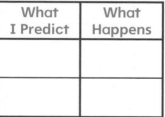

LOG ON ▶ LEARN IT Comprehension
www.macmillanmh.com

Comprehension

Genre
Fiction is a story with made-up characters and events.

Summarize
✔ **Make and Confirm Predictions**
As you read, use your Predictions Chart.

What I Predict	What Happens

Read to Find Out
How does Yoon feel about her new class?

My Name Is Yoon

by HELEN RECORVITS

illustrated by GABI SWIATKOWSKA

Award Winning Illustrator

My name is Yoon. I came here from Korea, a country far away.

It was not long after we **settled** in that my father called me to his side.

"Soon you will go to your new school. You must learn to print your name in English," he said. "Here. This is how it looks."

YOON

I **wrinkled** my nose. I did not like YOON. Lines. Circles. Each standing alone.

"My name looks happy in Korean," I said. "The symbols dance together.

"And in Korean my name means Shining Wisdom. I like the Korean way better."

"Well, you must learn to write it this way. Remember, even when you write in English, it still means Shining Wisdom."

I did not want to learn the new way. I wanted to go back home to Korea. I did not like America. Everything was different here. But my father handed me a pencil, and his eyes said Do-as-I-say. He showed me how to print every letter in the English alphabet. So I **practiced**, and my father was very pleased.

"Look," he called to my mother. "See how well our little Yoon does!"

"Yes," she said. "She will be a wonderful student!"

I wrinkled my nose.

Locate Facts
Locating facts helps us understand the story. What fact can you find about the meaning of Yoon's name?

My first day at school I sat quietly at my desk while the teacher talked about CAT. She wrote CAT on the chalkboard. She read a story about CAT. I did not know what her words meant, but I knew what the pictures said. She sang a song about CAT. It was a pretty song, and I tried to sing the words, too.

Later she gave me a paper with my name on it.

"Name. Yoon," she said. And she pointed to the empty lines underneath.

I did not want to write YOON. I wrote CAT instead. I wrote CAT on every line.

CAT CAT CAT

I wanted to be CAT. I wanted to hide in a corner. My mother would find me and **cuddle** up close to me. I would close my eyes and mew quietly.

The teacher looked at my paper. She shook her head and frowned. "So you are CAT?" she asked.

The ponytail girl sitting behind me giggled.

After school I said to my father, "We should go back to Korea. It is better there."

"Do not talk like that," he said. "America is your home now."

Make and Confirm Predictions
Do you predict that Yoon will make a friend in her new school? Use pictures or other details from the story to help make predictions.

I sat by the window and watched a little robin hop, hop in the yard. "He is all alone, too," I thought. "He has no friends. No one likes him."

Then I had a very good idea. "If I draw a picture for the teacher, then maybe she will like me."

It was the best bird I had ever drawn. "Look, Father," I said proudly.

"Oh, this makes me happy," he said. "Now do this." And he showed me how to print BIRD under the picture.

The next day at school the teacher handed me another YOON paper to print. But I did not want to print YOON. I wrote BIRD instead. I wrote BIRD on every line.

I wanted to be BIRD. I wanted to fly, fly back to Korea. I would fly to my nest, and I would tuck my head under my little brown wing.

The teacher looked at my paper. Again she shook her head. "So you are BIRD?" she asked.

Then I showed her my special robin drawing. I patted my red dress, and then I patted the red robin. I lowered my head and peeked up at her. The teacher smiled.

"How was school today, my daughter?" my mother asked.

"I think the teacher likes me a little," I said.

"Well, that is good!" my mother said.

"Yes, but at my school in Korea, I was my teacher's **favorite**. I had many friends. Here I am all alone."

"You must be **patient** with everyone, including yourself," my mother said. "You will be a fine student, and you will make many new friends here."

The next day at recess, I stood near the fence by myself. I watched the ponytail girl sitting on the swing. She watched me, too. Suddenly she jumped off the swing and ran over to me. She had a package in her hand. The wrapper said CUPCAKE. She opened it and gave me one. She giggled. I giggled, too.

When we were back in school, the teacher gave us more printing papers. I did not want to write YOON. I wrote CUPCAKE instead.

I wanted to be CUPCAKE. The children would clap their hands when they saw me. They would be excited. "CUPCAKE!" they would say. "Here is CUPCAKE!"

The teacher looked at my paper. "And today you are CUPCAKE!" she said. She smiled a very big smile. Her eyes said I-like-this-girl-Yoon.

After school I told my mother about my ponytail friend. I sang a new song for my father. I sang in English.

"You make us so proud, little Yoon," my mother said.

"Maybe America will be a good home," I thought. "Maybe different is good, too."

Make and Confirm Predictions
Has Yoon made a friend? What pictures or story details help you confirm your prediction?

The next day at school, I could hardly wait to print. And this time I wrote YOON on every line.

When my teacher looked at my paper, she gave me a big hug. "Aha! You are YOON!" she said.

Yes. I am YOON.

I write my name in English now. It still means Shining Wisdom.

Meet the Author and Illustrator

Helen Recorvits began writing stories when she was a young girl. When Helen was a teenager, she wrote for a small newspaper. Today she is a second-grade teacher as well as a writer. Helen says, "I love writing stories about people."

Gabi Swiatkowska won an award for her illustrations in this book. Gabi went to art school in Poland, and now lives in Brooklyn, New York. She knows what it is like to live in a new country.

Another book illustrated by Gabi Swiatkowska

LOG ON ▶ FIND OUT

Author Helen Recorvits
Illustrator Gabi Swiatkowska
www.macmillanmh.com

Arrowhawk

Lola M. Schaefer • ILLUSTRATED BY Gabi Swiatkowska

 Author's Purpose
Helen Recorvits tells a story about Yoon. Pretend that you are Yoon. Write a letter to your friends.

Comprehension Check

Retell the Story

Use the Retelling Cards to retell
the story.

Retelling Cards

Think and Compare

1. What was the first word Yoon wrote
   as her name? **Details**

2. How did you know that Yoon
   would like school at the end of the
   story? Use details from the story
   to support your answer. **Make and
   Confirm Predictions**

3. Yoon wanted to be a cat, a bird, and a cupcake.
   Use details from the story to explain why Yoon
   wanted to be something else. **Plot**

4. Yoon's mother talks about patience. What does
   the author want readers to learn? **Character**

5. Read "My New Home" on pages II0–III.
   How is Miguel like Yoon? How is he
   different? **Reading/Writing Across Texts**

What I Predict	What Happens

139

New Americans in Texas

By Ken Lee

Immigrants have come from other **countries** to live in Texas for many years. Immigrants are people who come to live in one country after they have left another country. Some immigrants come because they have family or friends in Texas. Others come because they want to work in America.

Immigrants come to Texas from many countries around the world. They come from countries as far away as Vietnam and India. They come from countries as close as Mexico and Guatemala.

Texas has a mix of people from all over the world. Because of this, people here have many different backgrounds and **cultures**. They have ideas and ways of life that they share with one another.

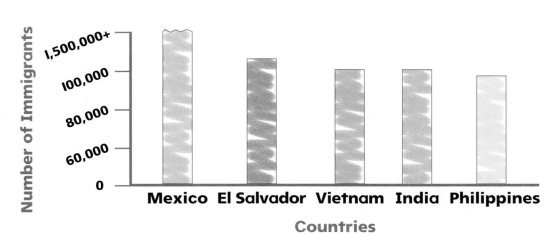

Countries Texas Immigrants Come From

Number of Immigrants

1,500,000+
100,000
80,000
60,000
0

Mexico El Salvador Vietnam India Philippines

Countries

This bar graph shows the countries that some immigrants come from. Use the bars to compare how many people come from each of these countries to live in Texas.

141

Immigrants coming to America have brought many interesting things with them. They have brought wonderful new kinds of music and clothes. Immigrants have also brought new words for Americans to speak and write. For example, *banana* and *poncho* are Spanish words.

Many tasty foods that we enjoy have been brought to the United States by immigrants, too. Have you ever eaten a grapefruit? Grapefruits came from the Caribbean and are now grown in Texas, too.

Grapefruits are a tasty kind of fruit that grow well in Texas.

Some of the music we listen to comes here from other countries. Reggae is music from Jamaica. A lot of popular music and dances are from Mexico.

Immigrants and people in the United States learn many new things from each other.

Mexican music is popular.

 Connect and Compare

1. From which country on the bar graph have the most immigrants come to Texas? **Bar Graphs**

2. Think about this article and *My Name Is Yoon*. What changes happen in the lives of immigrants when they come to a new country? Use details from the selections to help explain. **Reading/Writing Across Texts**

 Social Studies Activity

Use a map or globe to locate one of the countries listed on the graph. Research and write a paragraph about the country.

LOG ON ▶ FIND OUT Immigration
www.macmillanmh.com

Reading and Writing Connection

Writing

✓ **Sequence of Events**

Good writers use **sequence of events** to show the order that events happened.

I begin with the first thing I did at the beach.

The word <u>then</u> helps the reader understand the order of events.

July 4

What a super day! We went to the beach for my first 4th of July since moving to California! First Maggie and I made a huge sand castle. Then we collected shiny shells.

When it got late, we put on dry clothes and ate our dinner. We waited until it was dark for the fireworks. I told Dad that watching sparkling fireworks at the beach is the best!

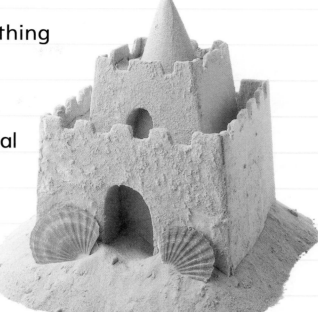

Your Writing Prompt

A journal entry tells about something
that has happened to you.

Think about a day that was special
for you. Why was it special?

Write a journal entry about
this special day.

Writer's Checklist

✓ My journal entry is written in the first
person, using words such as *I* and *my*.

☑ I use words such as *first* and *next* to make
the **sequence of events** clear.

✓ I include details that tell why my day
was special.

✓ I use the word *and* to combine sentences
with the same subject. I use punctuation
marks and capital letters correctly.

✓ **Review**

Character
Setting
Plot
Inflected Verbs

Puggles and Schnoodles

"Go on, Matty," Mrs. Min said. "What kind of dog is Mac?"

"A puggle," Matty repeated. Everyone giggled at the name.

Matty hadn't wanted to talk about her dog, Mac. She was new at school, and she wanted to fit in. She wanted to be like everyone else.

But it was Pet Week in school. She had to talk about Mac. And Mac was different. That was why the kids were giggling. They'd never heard of a puggle.

Matty was sitting by herself at lunch when Jenna sat down beside her. "I liked your dog, Matty," Jenna said. "But I've never heard of puggles before. What are they again?"

"A mix between a pug and a beagle," Matty answered.

"Do you want to see my dog? His name is Parker," Jenna said as she handed Matty a photo of her dog.

Matty had never seen a dog that looked like Parker. "What kind of dog is Parker?" she asked.

"He's a schnoodle," Jenna answered. "That's a mix between a schnauzer and a poodle." Both girls looked at each other and laughed.

After lunch, Matty and Jenna decided to write a report together. It was titled "Mixed Breed Dogs." It had a list that began with puggles and schnoodles.

Watching Whales

Becca's my best friend. That's why I said that I would go with her on a whale watch in the ocean.

"How exciting can it be to watch big fish swim?" I asked Becca as we headed to the ship.

"It's thrilling!" Becca said. "But whales aren't fish, Helena! They're mammals. They're the biggest mammals on Earth. They are twenty times larger than elephants!"

"But they're not as interesting as elephants," I said. "Did you ever watch elephants take a shower by spraying water from their trunks?"

"Yes," Becca replied as we got on the ship. "But whales spout water through their blowholes. Some spouts are 30 feet high!"

"Whales can even leap out of water," Becca told me as the ship started to move.

"Leap out of the water?" I asked as we found a place to stand by the railing. "Do you mean they leap through the air like monkeys?"

"Well, not like monkeys," Becca said. "But whales sometimes jump into the air. Or they'll push their tails into the air. Did you know that every whale's tail is different—just like every zebra's stripes are different?"

"Look at that," someone shouted as the ship glided farther out into the ocean. "A whale tail! See it over there?"

"Wow!" Becca yelled.

"WOW!" I yelled. "Ocean animals are exciting!"

149

Comprehension

Make and Confirm Predictions

- You can figure out what happens next in a story by using illustrations, titles, topics, sentences, or ideas. With a partner, read the paragraph below. Then talk about what might happen next. Explain to your partner how you made your prediction.

  The first day of school was scary for Jill. She just moved from another town. She missed her old friends and teachers. As Jill heard the bell ring, her new teacher took her by the hand.

 **Writing**

Write a Narrative

- Think about a funny event that happened when you were with a friend. Write about what happened. Be sure to include a beginning, a middle, and an end.

Word Study

Phonics

Consonant Digraphs *-ng, -ck, -ph, ch, tch, sh,* and *wh.*

- Read the following words: *rematch*, *chicken*, and *signing*. Point out the consonant digraph in each word. On a separate piece of paper, make three columns. Write the correct digraph at the top of each column. Then write other words you know that have these digraphs in the correct column.

- With a partner, review the digraphs *ch*, *tch*, *sh*, and *wh*. Include words that have these digraphs in a funny story. Circle each word.

Spelling

Words ending with *-an, -at, -ill, -ent, -ell, -ug*

- Write the following sentences on a separate piece of paper. Circle each word with an ending noted above.

  I have a tent.   Tell me a story.

  He gives the rope a tug.   Do you feel ill?

  I can jump high.   Give me the bat.

The
Big
Question

What heroes live
in your community?

LOG
ON ▶ VIEW IT

Theme Video
Community Heroes
www.macmillanmh.com

What heroes live in your community?

Heroes face difficult situations with strength, courage, and wisdom. Heroes can be people we see every day who work at home. They can also be people in the community who work to make people's lives better. Heroes can be grownups or children. Some heroes have strong bodies to fight fires, carry sick people, or rescue people in danger. Others heroes have strong minds that they use to teach people things they need to know, cure sick people, or invent new things to make work easier or safer.

Research Activities

During the unit you will gather information about community heroes. As a class we will make a list of topics and create open-ended questions about community heroes. Choose one hero and topic to research. Then create a dramatic play about that hero's work.

Keep Track of Ideas

As you read, keep track of all you learn about community heroes. Use the **Four-Door Foldable**. On the top left tab, write Heroes. On the top right tab, write Who Are Heroes? On the bottom left tab, write Where Do Heroes Live? On the bottom right tab, write What Do Heroes Do? Write facts that you learn each week in the appropriate section.

FOLDABLES
Study Organizer

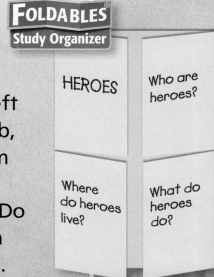

HEROES

Who are heroes?

Where do heroes live?

What do heroes do?

Digital Learning

LOG ON ▶ FIND OUT www.macmillanmh.com

StudentWorks *Plus*
Interactive Student Book

- **Research Roadmap**
  Follow a step-by-step guide to complete your research project.

Online Resources

- Topic Finder and Other Research Tools
- Videos and Virtual Field Trips
- Photos and Drawings for Presentations
- Related Articles and Web Resources
- Web Site Links

People and Places

Bessie Coleman

Bessie Coleman (1892–1926) was born in Atlanta, TX. She attended aviation school in France and became the first African American licensed pilot in the United States.

FAMILY
HEROES

Talk About It

Think about what it means to be a hero. Describe someone in your family who is a hero.

LOG ON ▶ **VIEW IT**

Oral Language Activities
Family Heroes
www.macmillanmh.com

Vocabulary

exclaimed

concern

vendors

figure

collection

✔ Context Clues

To clarify an unfamiliar word in a story, use context clues in sentences to help you figure out the meaning.

The statue showed the *figure* of a man. *Figure* means "form" or "shape."

---

e-mail

Write Send Reply Print Delete @ Addresses

From: gram@example.com
To: aki@example.com

Dear Aki,

It was so nice to visit you in Michigan, but I'm glad to be back home in Japan. I showed Grandfather pictures from your soccer game. "Look at her shin guards and gloves!" he **exclaimed**. He sounded very surprised. I explained that you are a goalie. It's your job to guard the goal and keep the other team from scoring. Grandfather's **concern** is for your safety. He is worried that you might get hurt. Now he knows that what you wear helps keep you safe.

Love,
Grandmother

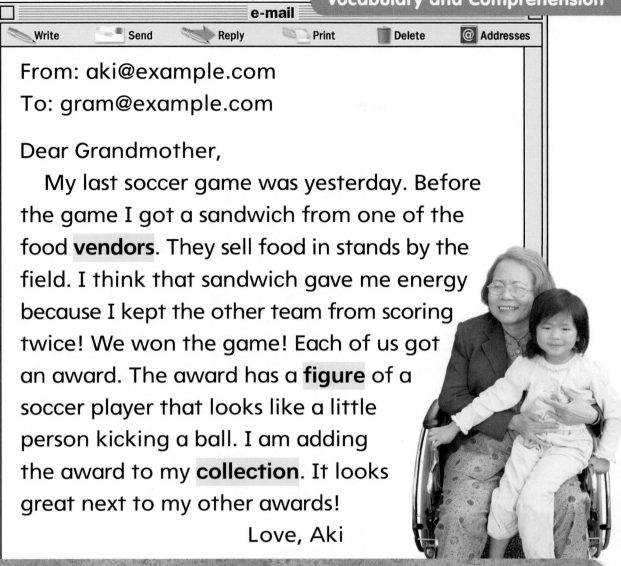

e-mail

Write   Send   Reply   Print   Delete   @ Addresses

From: aki@example.com
To: gram@example.com

Dear Grandmother,

   My last soccer game was yesterday. Before the game I got a sandwich from one of the food **vendors**. They sell food in stands by the field. I think that sandwich gave me energy because I kept the other team from scoring twice! We won the game! Each of us got an award. The award has a **figure** of a soccer player that looks like a little person kicking a ball. I am adding the award to my **collection**. It looks great next to my other awards!

                                    Love, Aki

Reread for **Comprehension**

Reread

Character, Setting, Plot Rereading parts of a story can help you understand the characters, setting, and plot. Reread the e-mails and use the Story Map to describe the characters and how the setting and plot change their actions and feelings (including problems and solutions) in the beginning, middle, and end.

Characters
Setting
Beginning
↓
Middle
↓
End

LOG ON ▶ LEARN IT   Comprehension
www.macmillanmh.com

Comprehension

Genre
Fiction is a story with made-up characters and events.

Reread
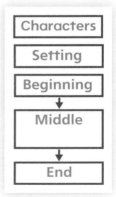
Character, Setting, Plot
As you read, use your Story Map.

Characters
Setting
Beginning
↓
Middle
↓
End

Read to Find Out
Who are Babu and Bernardi? Why do they get along so well?

Babu's Song

by
Stephanie Stuve-Bodeen

illustrated by
Aaron Boyd

Bernardi ran hard, kicking the ball toward the goal. His arms pumping and his heart racing, he didn't care that he was the only boy on the field not wearing a school uniform.

He loved soccer and his one **concern** was making a goal. With a final kick so powerful that it knocked him on his back, Bernardi sent the ball flying past the goalie and into the net.

Bernardi lay on the grassy field, catching his breath. A boy helped him up, then ran after the others going into the school. Bernardi wished he could go to school like the other children. He liked to learn, and thought he could be a good student. Besides, then he could play soccer every day, not just when the schoolboys needed an extra player. Bernardi lived with his grandfather, Babu, and they did not have enough money for school.

Slowly Bernardi walked home.

165

When Bernardi walked in, Babu gave him a hug. This was how he said hello, because an illness had taken his voice a long time ago.

"Hello, Babu," Bernardi said. "I made a goal today." Bernardi loved telling Babu his soccer stories.

Babu held up a **figure** made of wood. He pulled a string, and the figure's jointed arms and legs popped up and down, making Bernardi laugh. Babu was a toy maker. He had only to look at an object and he knew what toy it would become, such as an airplane from a tin can or a whistle from a scrap of wood.

After Babu made his toys Bernardi would sell them. Together they made enough money to live on.

Character, Setting, Plot
How does the setting affect Bernardi's feelings and actions?

Babu made tea for Bernardi and himself. After they finished Bernardi took an old bag from beside the door, waved good-bye to Babu, and set off for the market. As he walked, Bernardi hummed a tune. It was a song that Babu had sung when he had his voice. Humming it made Bernardi wish Babu could still speak.

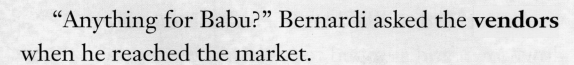

"Anything for Babu?" Bernardi asked the **vendors** when he reached the market.

The vendors gave Bernardi bits of string or paper, anything that Babu might be able to use to make his toys. Mama Valentina, who sold salt, called to Bernardi. She handed him a plastic gunnysack. Bernardi thanked her as he stuffed it into his bag, even though he didn't think Babu could use it.

As Bernardi walked home, he passed a shop downtown and stopped to look in the window. There among the bright bolts of cloth and shiny pots was a new soccer ball. It was just what he had always wanted. Bernardi pressed his face against the window and looked at the price. It was more than it cost to go to school!

Slowly Bernardi backed away from the window. He did not hum as he walked home.

That evening Babu and Bernardi ate beans and rice by the light of the kerosene lamp. Babu put something by Bernardi's plate. Bernardi picked it up and held it closer to the light. It looked like a tin of lard. He opened the lid and heard a small tinkling.

"A music box!" Bernardi **exclaimed**, and listened again. It was rough and tinny, but he recognized the tune. It was Babu's song.

Bernardi hugged Babu, and together they listened to the music. That night, for the first time in many nights, Bernardi fell asleep listening to Babu's song.

The next Saturday was a busy one for
Bernardi, as it was the day he sold toys to
tourists. He set up shop on his favorite corner
downtown, arranging the toys on the curb.

Bernardi cranked the music box and
listened to Babu's song tinkle out. He had
sold a few things when a woman picked up the
music box. She asked how much it was, but
Bernardi said it wasn't for sale.

The woman did not give up. She told Bernardi that she wanted the music box for her **collection**, but still Bernardi shook his head. The woman held out a handful of money. Bernardi's eyes widened. It would be more than enough to buy the ball in the store window.

Bernardi picked up the music box. He thought about the brand-new ball and how it would feel when he kicked it. Surely Babu could make another music box.

Bernardi swallowed hard and took the money.

After Bernardi sold all the toys he did not go home. He took the money and headed for the shops down the street.

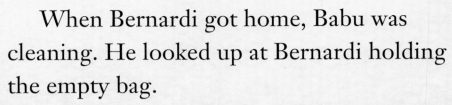

When Bernardi got home, Babu was cleaning. He looked up at Bernardi holding the empty bag.

"I sold everything, Babu!" Bernardi said, trying to sound cheerful, but then a tear rolled down his face. Babu went over to Bernardi. He wiped his grandson's face and waited. He knew Bernardi would tell him what was wrong.

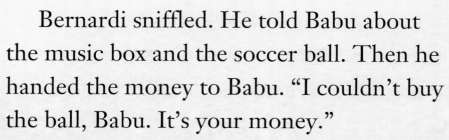

Bernardi sniffled. He told Babu about the music box and the soccer ball. Then he handed the money to Babu. "I couldn't buy the ball, Babu. It's your money."

Babu patted Bernardi's head. Then he placed the money in Bernardi's hand and held it, to show him that the money belonged to both of them.

179

Bernardi hung his head. "I don't want the ball anymore." He held out the money. "Take it, Babu. You decide what to do with the money."

Babu took the money and looked thoughtfully at Bernardi for a long time. Then he broke into a smile, signaled to Bernardi to wait, and walked out the door.

Bernardi sat quietly in the room as he waited for Babu. He wished he still had the music box. How could he have sold it?

Bernardi was sitting in the lamplight when Babu returned holding a paper bag. Babu pulled out a package and handed it to Bernardi.

Bernardi choked back a sob. He untied the string and pulled back the brown paper. His eyes opened wide when he saw what was inside. It was a school uniform!

Bernardi looked at Babu. "You paid for me to go to school?"

Babu nodded. Bernardi jumped up and hugged his grandfather.

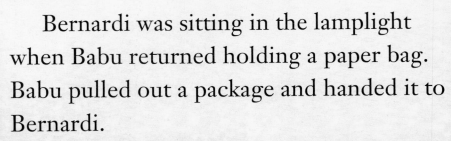

Characters, Setting, Plot
Think about the story's plot. Use details to describe the beginning, middle, and end of the story.

While Bernardi held the new uniform to his chest, Babu went back outside. He returned holding something behind his back. With a flourish Babu held out a soccer ball made from string and Mama Valentina's gunnysack.

Bernardi put down his uniform and held the ball. He bounced it on one knee and it felt like the real thing.

"Thank you, Babu. It's wonderful!" Bernardi said to his grandfather and gave him a hug. Babu beamed. Bernardi decided that the ball was even better than the real thing.

Babu pulled one more surprise from the paper bag. It was an empty lard tin. As Babu began to make another music box, Bernardi put the water on the stove to boil. Then Bernardi hummed Babu's song as they sat in the lamplight and waited for their tea.

Exploring People and Places with Stephanie and Aaron

STEPHANIE STUVE-BODEEN once lived in a village in Tanzania, Africa. Tanzania is where this story takes place. While she was there, Stephanie lived near a school. It was like the one Bernardi wants to go to.

AARON BOYD knew he wanted to be an illustrator when he was just six years old. He would go to the library and study all the picture books. "I liked trying to read the story through just the pictures," he says. "It seemed very magical to me, making a story with pictures."

Other books illustrated by Aaron Boyd

 **FIND OUT**

Author Stephanie Stuve-Bodeen
Illustrator Aaron Boyd
www.macmillanmh.com

Author's Purpose
The author tells a story about a soccer ball that is special to a boy. Write a description of something that is special to you.

✔ Comprehension Check

Retell the Story

Use the Retelling Cards
to retell the story.

Retelling Cards

Think and Compare

1. What does Bernardi love to do? Facts

2. When the woman wanted the music box
   for her **collection**, why did Bernardi sell it
   to her? Use story details to explain. Plot

Characters
Setting
Beginning
↓
Middle
↓
End

3. How do the different settings affect
   Bernardi's feelings and actions? Use
   details from the text to support your answer.
   Character, Setting, Plot

4. How does Babu help Bernardi change?
   How does the author show this change?
   Character

5. Compare Bernardi's life with his
   grandfather to Aki's with her
   grandmother in "E-mails from
   Other Places" on pages 158–159.
   Reading/Writing Across Texts

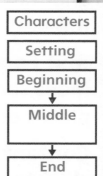

Where in the World Is Tanzania?

by Jeff Mateo

Africa is the second largest continent. It is so big that the United States could fit in it three times! Africa is between the Atlantic and Indian Oceans. It is south of the Mediterranean Sea. Africa has the hottest **climate** on Earth. This means the weather is hotter there than on any other continent.

There are 53 countries in Africa. Tanzania is a country in southeast Africa. Dodoma is its **capital** city. This is where the government is found. It is a **democracy**. This means that the people can vote for their leaders.

Tanzania has three types of land. The coastal area is long and flat. It is found along the Indian Ocean.

The plateau is large and flat. It is found in the middle of the country. It is covered in trees and tall grasses. A large part of it is the Great Rift Valley.

The mountains are in the west. The highest point is on Mount Kilimanjaro, which stands more than 19,000 feet tall.

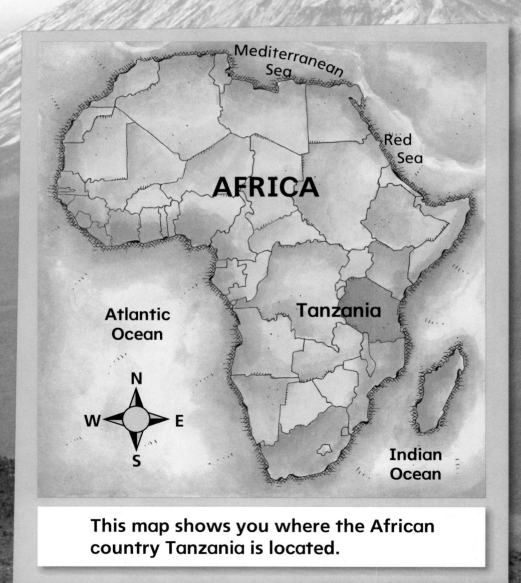

This map shows you where the African country Tanzania is located.

191

More than 33 million people live in Tanzania. There are 120 different tribes of people and each has its own customs and beliefs. The national language is Kiswahili. Tanzanians may speak English as well as the languages of their tribes.

Each tribe, such as the Makonde and Masai, has its own traditions and dances. Visitors come to learn about the people and watch the dances. The dances tell exciting stories.

Many people in Tanzania are farmers and miners. They dig minerals and gems, such as gold and diamonds, out of the ground.

Other Tanzanians help the tourists who come to visit the country. They work in hotels and give tours. Some Tanzanians make and sell crafts to tourists. Tourism is a big business in Tanzania. People come from all over the world to see the amazing wildlife.

Tanzania has many wild animals, such as lions, zebras, giraffes, and baboons. Many live in national parks, which are animal sanctuaries. The workers help protect the animals and the places where they live.

 Connect and Compare

1. Which ocean is next to Tanzania? **Map**

2. Think about this article and *Babu's Song*. What new information does the article give you about life in Tanzania? **Reading/Writing Across Texts**

 Social Studies Activity

Research Tanzania using a different source. Use the table of contents, index, and headings to locate information. Record a list of facts you learn.

 **Social Studies** Africa
www.macmillanmh.com

Reading and Writing Connection

✔ **Sequence of Events**

Good writers use **sequence of events** to tell story events in the correct order.

I tell what Aunt Dora does in the correct order.

The words <u>at the end</u> make the order of events clear.

My Hero Aunt

My Aunt Dora helps out at a pet shelter in our town. The dogs bark and wag their tails when they see her. The first thing Aunt Dora does is take the dogs for a walk. After their walk, Aunt Dora gives the dogs a bath. She gets very wet but says it is lots of fun! At the end of her visit Aunt Dora gives each dog food and water. I am so proud of Aunt Dora. She is a hero to the dogs at the shelter!

Your Writing Prompt

A family member can be a hero in many different ways.

Think about a family member who has done something heroic.

Write a story about what that person does.

Writer's Checklist

 My writing is focused on a family hero.

 My writing includes a clear sequence of events.

 I include details that describe why I am proud of the person.

 I use nouns to name people, places, and things. My sentences are complete and punctuated correctly.

Local Heroes

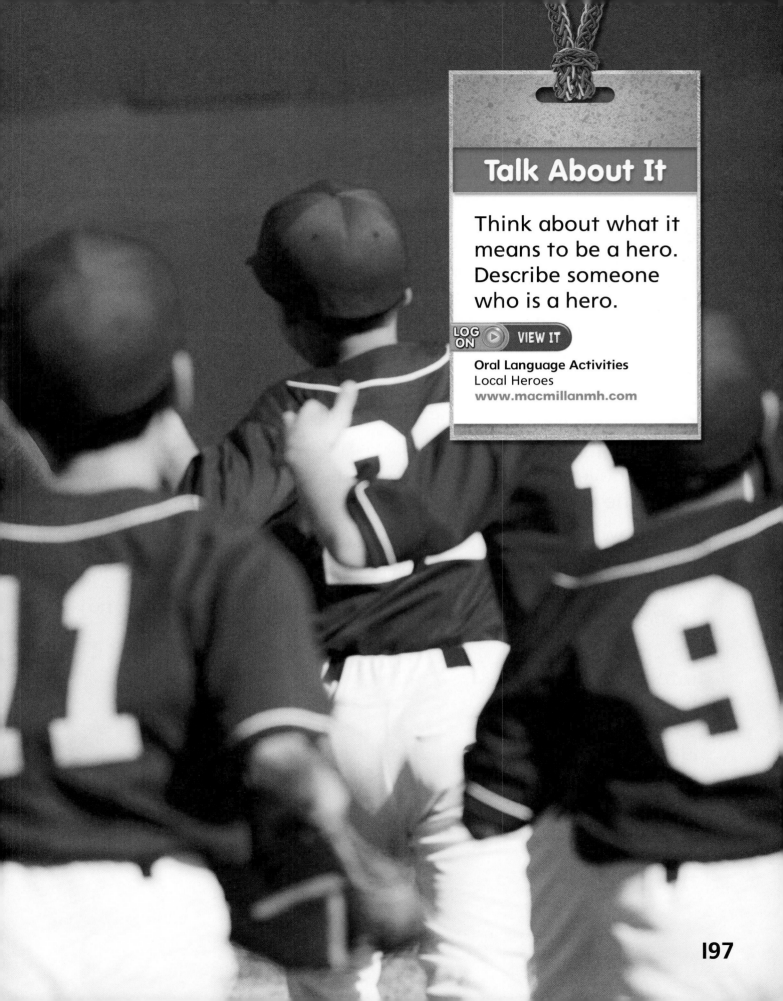

Talk About It

Think about what it means to be a hero. Describe someone who is a hero.

LOG ON ▶ VIEW IT

Oral Language Activities
Local Heroes
www.macmillanmh.com

197

SLUE-FOOT SUE AND PECOS BILL

Vocabulary

respected

rattled

tangle

commotion

shivering

advice

✔ **Context Clues**

Multiple-meaning words have more than one meaning.

The blowing wind *rattled* the windows.

The loud noise *rattled* the speaker.

To **clarify** information in a story, use **context clues** to figure out the meaning of the word.

Slue-Foot Sue was a strong and smart Texas woman who could do anything she wanted. Everyone **respected** her. They all thought she was a great gal.

One day Sue hopped on a big catfish and took a ride on the Rio Grande. They went so fast downriver that the branches on the nearby trees **rattled**, making loud, sharp noises.

Pecos Bill was riding his horse near the river. Bill's horse was so strong that he could ride his way out of any **tangle**, no matter how tricky the mess was.

When Bill heard the **commotion** coming from the river, he stopped and thought, "What is that loud noise? Who is causing the fuss?"

Bill turned and saw Sue. She spied Bill and his horse on the riverbank, so she jumped off the catfish. Sue was **shivering** and shaking from the cold water. "My name is Slue-Foot Sue," she said. "You sure have a mighty fine horse."

Bill replied, "I'm Pecos Bill. He is a great horse, but he only likes me to ride him. I wouldn't want you to get hurt."

Sue listened to Bill's **advice**. The words he told her made sense, so she did not ride his horse. From that time on, though, they shared many fun adventures.

Reread for **Comprehension**

Monitor Comprehension: Reread

Cause and Effect Rereading parts of a story is an **adjustment** you can make to help you understand causes and their effects. A cause is why something happens. An effect is what happens. Reread the story and use the chart to figure out why Slue-Foot Sue does not ride Pecos Bill's horse.

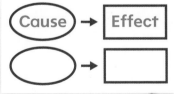

Cause → Effect

LOG ON ▶ LEARN IT Comprehension
www.macmillanmh.com

199

Comprehension

Genre
A **Folktale** is a made-up story that takes place long ago.

Reread
✓ **Cause and Effect**
As you read, fill in your Cause and Effect Chart.

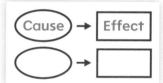

Read to Find Out
How does Doña Flor help her neighbors?

DOÑA FLOR

A Tall Tale About a Giant Woman with a Great Big Heart

By Pat Mora
Illustrated by Raul Colón

Award Winning Author

201

Every winter morning when the sun opened one eye, Doña Flor grabbed a handful of snow from the top of a nearby mountain. *"Brrrrrrrr,"* she said, rubbing the snow on her face to wake up.

Long, long ago, when Flor was a baby, her mother sang to her in a voice sweet as river music. When Flor's mother sang to her corn plants, they grew tall as trees, and when she sang to her baby, her sweet flower, well, Flor grew and grew, too.

Some children laughed at her because she was different. "*¡Mira!* Look! Big Foot!" they called when she walked by.

"Flor talks funny," they whispered, because Flor spoke to butterflies and grasshoppers. She spoke every language, even rattler.

But soon Flor's friends and neighbors asked her for help. Children late for school asked, "*Por favor,* Flor, could you give us a ride?" She took just one of her giant steps and was at the school door. Of course, the *escuela* shook and the windows rattled.

When Flor finally stopped growing, she built her own house, *una casa* big as a mountain and open as a canyon. She scooped a handful of dirt and made herself a valley for mixing clay, straw, and water. She added some *estrellas*. The stars made the adobe shine. When she worked, Flor sang, and birds came and built nests in her hair. Flor wanted everyone to feel at home in her house. *"Mi casa es su casa,"* she said to people, animals, and plants, so they knew they were always welcome. Everyone called her *Doña* Flor because they respected her.

No one needed an alarm clock in Doña Flor's pueblo. When her hands, wide as plates, started pat-pat-patting tortillas, everyone in the village woke up. So her neighbors would have plenty to eat, she stacked her tortillas on the huge rock table in front of her house.

Flor's tortillas were the biggest, bestest tortillas in the whole wide world. People used the extra ones as roofs. *Mmmm*, the houses smelled corn-good when the sun was hot. In the summer, the children floated around the pond on tortilla rafts.

One warm spring day, while a family of lizards swept her house, Doña Flor brought out her stacks of fresh tortillas. Nobody came. *Hmmmmmmm*, thought Flor. She started knocking on doors and calling to her neighbors.

"*¿Qué pasa?* What's the matter?" she asked, bending down to peer into their small doors to see where they were hiding.

"*¿El puma!*" they whispered. "The children have heard a huge mountain lion circling the village. Listen!"

Flor listened, and sure enough, she heard a terrible "*Rrrr-oarrr!*"

Doña Flor and her animal friends went out looking for the huge *gato*, but they couldn't find it. That night, she carried her tired friends, the coyotes and rabbits, back home. But just as she started to tuck them in and read them a good-night story, they all heard, "*Rrrr-oarrr!*"

"Where is that darn cat?" asked Flor, but the scared animals were shaking and shivering under their sheets. She gave each a giant kiss.

SMACK! The sound echoed and woke the grumpy wind, who stormed up and down the hills a-grumblin' and a-growlin'. That night, the wind got so angry that he blew the trees and houses first to the left and then to the right, again to the left and then to the right.

Cause and Effect
What causes the wind to wake up? What was the effect? Use details from the story to support your answer.

Now, Doña Flor liked her sleep, so she wasn't smiling when she heard the wind spinnin' round and around the village. Together, the wind and the giant cat roared all night, and nobody got much sleep.

As the sun rose, Flor's neighbors, shaking at the commotion, peered out their windows. Tired-looking Flor was giving that wind a big hug to quiet him down. Then she started her morning chores.

Doña Flor had work to do. But first she looked around the village. Where were her neighbors? Then she heard, *"Rrrr-oarrr! Rrrr-oarrr!"*

Flor stomped off to find the puma that was bothering her *amigos*.

Exhausted by afternoon, Doña Flor still hadn't found that cat, so she sat outside the library for a rest. She was too big to fit inside, so she just reached in the window for books. You see, Flor was probably the fastest reader ever. Why, she could read the whole encyclopedia in five minutes. She liked to sit in the shade and read stories and poems nice and slow to the children and animals that climbed all over her soft body. Today, she called and called, and finally the children came, but they were scared.

What can I do to cheer my friends up? wondered Flor as she saw their frightened faces. She thought and thought. Now, Flor knew that her village needed *un río,* a river, so to make her neighbors happy, Doña Flor scratched a new riverbed with her thumb. When the water trickled down the stones for the first time, Flor called out, "Just listen to that! Isn't that the prettiest sound you've ever heard?" She smiled, and her smile was about as big as her tortillas, but today her neighbors could barely smile back. They were too worried about the mountain lion, and sure enough, suddenly there was a terrible *"Rrrr-oarrr! Rrrr-oarrr!"*

That's it! thought Doña Flor, and again she stomped off to look for the giant puma, but she still couldn't find him. She went home to think and work in her garden. It was like a small forest on the edge of the *pueblo*, a tangle of poppies, morning glories, roses, luscious tomatoes, and *chiles*. Whatever she planted grew so fast, you could hear the roots spreading at night. Her neighbors used the sunflowers as bright yellow umbrellas. She gave the school band her hollyhocks to use as trumpets. The music smelled like spring.

"My plants grow that big because I sing to them like my mother did," Doña Flor told the children when they came three at a time to carry home an ear of corn. But today, the children ran home when they heard, *"Rrrr-oarrr!"* The sound rattled all the plates in the pueblo. Flor's neighbors' teeth started rattling, too.

Where is that big monster gato? Doña Flor wondered. The smell of roses helped Flor think, so she went inside and took a long, hot bubble bath. Everyone knew Doña Flor was thinking when bubbles that smelled like roses began to rise from her chimney.

I know, thought Flor, *I'll go to my animal friends for help.* She stomped off again, and she started asking because, remember, she spoke every language, even rattler.

"Go quietly to the tallest mesa," said the deer.

"Vaya silencios-s-s-amente a la mes-s-s-a mas-s-s alta," hissed the snake.

"Go quietly to the tallest mesa," whispered the rabbits.

Knowing that animals are mighty smart,
Doña Flor followed their advice. She walked
very, very softly up to the tallest mesa. She
looked around carefully for the giant cat. Then
right near her she heard, *"Rrrr-oarrr! Rrrr-
oarrr!"* Flor jumped so high, she bumped into
the sun and gave him a black eye.

Flor looked around. All she saw was the
back of a cute little puma. She watched him
very quietly. Doña Flor began to tiptoe toward
the puma when all of a sudden he roared into
a long, hollow log. The sound became a huge
"Rrrr-oarrr!" that echoed down into the valley.

Now, the little puma thought the loud noise was so funny that he rolled on his back and started laughing and laughing—until he saw big Doña Flor.

Aha! thought Flor. "Are you the *chico* who's causing all the trouble?" she asked. The little puma tried to look very fierce. His eyes sizzled with angry sparks. He opened his mouth wide, and his teeth glinted. He roared his meanest roar. *"Rrrr-oarrr!"* he growled, but without the log, the growl wasn't really very fierce.

Doña Flor just smiled at that brave cat and said, "Why, you're just a kitten to me, Pumito," and she bent down and scratched that puma behind the ears, and she whispered to him in cat talk until that cat began to purr and *purrrrrrrrr.* Pumito began to lick Flor's face with his wet tongue.

Cause and Effect
What is the effect of the little puma purring into the log?

Suddenly Flor heard a new noise. *"Doña Flor, ¿dónde estás?* Where are you?" called her worried neighbors. Even though they were frightened, they had all come, holding hands, looking for her.

"Meet my new *amigo,*" said Doña Flor, smiling at her thoughtful neighbors.

That evening, Flor plucked a star the way she always did and plunked it on the tallest tree so her friends in the *pueblo* could find their way home. She plucked *una estrella* to put above her door, too. Even the stars could hear Doña Flor humming.

Flor liked a fresh bed, so she reached up and filled her arms with clouds smelling of flowery breezes. She shaped the clouds into a soft, deep bed and into hills of puffy pillows. *"Mmmm,"* said Flor as she snuggled in the clouds.

"Tonight, I'm very tired after my adventure
with the giant cat, right, Pumito?" chuckled
Doña Flor. All the animals snuggled down with
her, and Pumito stretched out over her big toes.

Standing Tall with PAT AND RAUL

PAT MORA likes to create characters like Doña Flor. She enjoyed writing this original tall tale because the character of Doña Flor is strong yet kind. She also speaks more than one language—just like Pat! Pat would love to have Doña Flor as her own neighbor and local hero.

RAUL COLÓN likes creating different kinds of art. He started drawing comic books when he was a child. Raul has won awards for his beautiful illustrations.

Other books written by Pat Mora

LOG ON ► FIND OUT

Author Pat Mora
Illustrator Raul Colón
www.macmillanmh.com

✔ Author's Purpose

Pat Mora tells about a character who helps others. Think of someone in your community who helps you. Write a paragraph about that person.

✔ Comprehension Check

Retell the Story

Use the Retelling Cards to retell the story.

Retelling Cards

Think and Compare

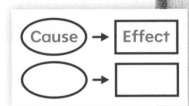

Cause	→	Effect
	→	

1. What makes the children laugh at Doña Flor? **Details**

2. What causes Doña Flor's neighbors to be afraid? What effect does it have on Doña Flor? Use details from the story to support your answer. **Cause and Effect**

3. How does Doña Flor feel about the world around her? **Make Inferences**

4. What might the author want readers to learn from Doña Flor? **Author's Purpose**

5. Pat Mora also wrote *David's New Friends*. How is the setting of *Doña Flor* like the one in *David's New Friends*? How are they different? How are the stories' plots alike and different? **Reading/Writing Across Texts**

Henrietta Chamberlain King

By Linda B. Ross

Henrietta King was an important person in Texas history. She was an excellent rancher and a woman who gave back to her community.

Henrietta and her husband, Richard, owned a ranch on the Santa Gertrudis Creek. Henrietta cared for her five children. She also managed the **education** and housing of all the Mexican American families who worked at the King Ranch.

In 1925, the King Ranch was 1,173,000 acres. It was larger than the state of Rhode Island!

King Ranch Grows

In 1885, Henrietta's husband died. At that time she owned 500,000 **acres** of land. Henrietta and her son-in-law kept the ranch going. They raised a new and stronger breed of cattle called Santa Gertrudis cattle.

As the King Ranch grew, Henrietta **donated** more to the community. She gave 75,000 acres to build a railroad between St. Louis and Mexico. She gave land and money to build schools, hospitals, and churches. Henrietta died in 1925, but she will always be remembered for her good work.

Henrietta Chamberlain King was born in 1832 and died in 1925.

 Connect and Compare

1. How large was the King Ranch in 1925? **Photographs and Captions**

2. Think about this biography and Doña Flor. What made Henrietta a local hero like Doña Flor? **Reading/Writing Across Texts**

 Social Studies Activity

Research a hero who has helped your community. Make a poster that describes this person.

LOG ON ▶ FIND OUT   **Social Studies** Heroes
www.macmillanmh.com

233

Reading and Writing Connection

This important detail tells the reader where to go.

This important detail explains what to do next.

How to Apply for a Library Card

1. Go to the library with a grown-up.

2. Tell a librarian that you would like a library card.

3. Fill out the forms that the librarian gives you.

4. Use your new library card to borrow great books!

Your Writing Prompt

There are many ways people can help themselves and others.

Think about a time when you helped yourself or someone else.

Write a set of directions that explains how you helped.

Writer's Checklist

✓ My writing is about how to help myself or someone else.

✓ My directions are numbered to show the order of steps for the reader to do.

☑ I include important details that make the information clear.

✓ I use a capital letter to begin each sentence. I use plural nouns correctly.

Talk About It

Think of ways we can remember community heroes.

LOG ON ▶ **VIEW IT**

Oral Language Activities
Remembering Community Heroes
www.macmillanmh.com

Remembering

COMMUNITY
HEROES

Vocabulary

state
independence
landmark
symbol
government

Texans celebrate the state holiday with parades and festivals near the capitol.

Lone Star Celebration

March 2 is a **state** holiday in Texas. It is called Texas Independence Day. Before March 2, 1836, Texas was part of Mexico. On that date Texas leaders said Texas was a separate country. It was independent, or free, of Mexico. Ten years later Texas became part of the United States.

Today Texans honor their **independence** with parades and festivals. Some people hold "Happy Birthday, Texas" parties. On this day Texans show pride in their state!

Our Capital's Capitol

The United States Capitol is in Washington, D.C. The Capitol is the home of the United States Congress. Our senators and representatives meet there to pass laws. The Capitol building was started in 1793, but not completely finished until 1960.

The United States Capitol is in Washington, D.C.

Every year about five million people from all over the world visit the Capitol. They can watch members of the Senate and the House of Representatives at work. Visitors can also see statues and paintings and visit all 540 rooms in the building.

The Capitol's roof is a giant dome. Some people think the dome is America's most famous **landmark**. It is a **symbol** of our **government** and its laws.

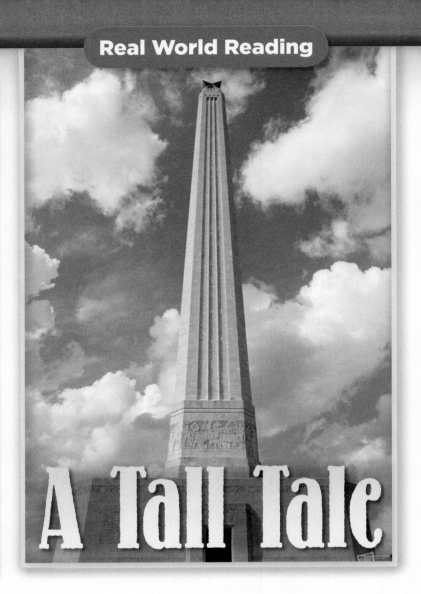

Comprehension

Genre
Expository text gives information about real people, places, and events.

Read Ahead

Main Idea and Details
The main idea is the most important idea in an article. Details and facts give more information.

A Tall Tale

INDEPENDENCE FOR TEXAS

The San Jacinto (SAN juh–SIN–toh) Monument rises 570 feet into the Texas sky. At the top of the monument is a huge star. It is a **symbol** of Texas, the Lone Star State. Inside the monument is a museum. It tells the story of the Battle of San Jacinto. This amazing **landmark** stands on the spot where that battle was fought.

240

Texas was once part of Mexico. Many people who lived in Texas came from the United States. They wanted Texas to break away from Mexico. In 1835, Texans fought against Mexico to form their own country. The Mexican army defeated the Texans in some battles. At San Jacinto the Texans won a big victory. Mexico had to give Texas its **independence**. These people are heroes to the community.

The huge monument tells the story of the Battle of San Jacinto.

Workers from the community build each piece of the monument by hand.

Building the Monument

The Texas **government** began building the San Jacinto Monument in 1936. First, workers had to make the base. It took 57 hours to pour the concrete for the foundation. After the base was ready, stones were placed on top to make the tower. Each stone weighed as much as 8,000 pounds. Work on the monument ended in 1939, but the hard work is always remembered. The people who made it possible were community worker heroes.

The metal front doors of the San Jacinto Monument tell a story. The doors show six flags that flew over the **state** at different times. They are the flags of Spain, France, Mexico, the Republic of Texas, the Confederate States of America, and the United States. They show that Texas history is linked to world history.

The metal doors to the monument show the different flags flown over Texas.

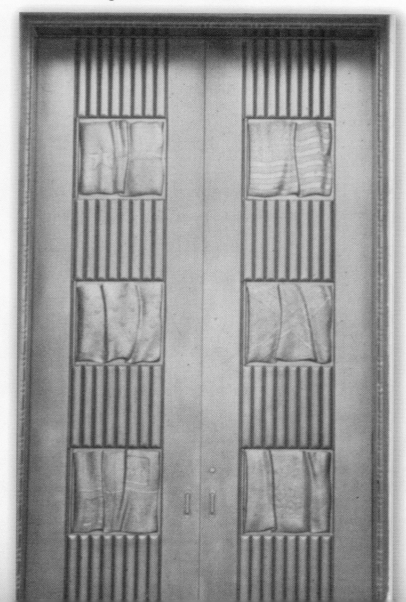

Think and Compare

1. Where is the monument located?

2. Why was the monument built?

3. Use facts and other details from the text to state the main idea.

4. Think about "Lone Star Celebration" and this article. Why are Texas Independence Day and the San Jacinto Monument important to Texans?

A Day to Remember

❶ What is the meaning of Memorial Day? It is all about remembering. A memorial is something that keeps a memory alive. On Memorial Day we remember our soldiers who have died.

❷ This holiday used to be called Decoration Day. It began on May 30, 1868. Every May 30, people decorated the graves of soldiers who died in the Civil War. In 1888, the name of the holiday was changed to Memorial Day. It honors men and women who have died in all wars. Now Memorial Day is celebrated on the last Monday of May. People still decorate the graves of soldiers on Memorial Day. Some communities have parades to remember local soldiers.

244

DIRECTIONS
Decide which is the best answer to each question.

Read the first sentence of the summary below.

> Summary of "A Day to Remember"
>   Memorial Day is an important
> American holiday.

1   Which set of sentences best completes the summary?

(A) The first time it was celebrated was in 1868. Memorial Day helps us remember the Civil War.

(B) We use a memorial to remember someone or something special. Sometimes we use decorations.

(C) On this day we remember the soldiers who have died for our country. We celebrate this national holiday in May.

(D) People decorate the graves of soldiers. Some communities have parades for local soldiers.

2   Before 1888, Memorial Day was called —

(A) Community Day

(B) Decoration Day

(C) Parade Day

(D) May Day

3   Today we celebrate Memorial Day on the —

(A) first Monday in May

(B) last day in May

(C) weekends in May

(D) last Monday in May

Write to a Prompt

Trina wrote about a time when she helped someone.

My story has details about Mrs. Clay.

Mrs. Clay and the Snowy Day

Mrs. Clay is our neighbor and our friend. She cannot do all the things she used to do. Last winter there was a big snowstorm. The street and the grass all turned white.

My big brother and I wanted to help Mrs. Clay. We asked her if we could shovel her driveway. It was hard work! When we were finished, Mrs. Clay invited us inside her house for some hot chocolate. We were glad we had helped our friend.

Writing Prompt

Respond in writing to the prompt below. Review the hints below before and after you write.

Write about a time when you helped someone.

Writing Hints

- ☑ Remember to write about a time when you helped someone.

- ☑ Plan your writing by organizing your ideas.

- ☑ Include important details to support your ideas.

- ☑ Check that each sentence you write helps the reader understand your writing.

- ☑ Use correct spelling, capitalization, punctuation, grammar, and sentences.

- ☑ Review and edit your writing.

247

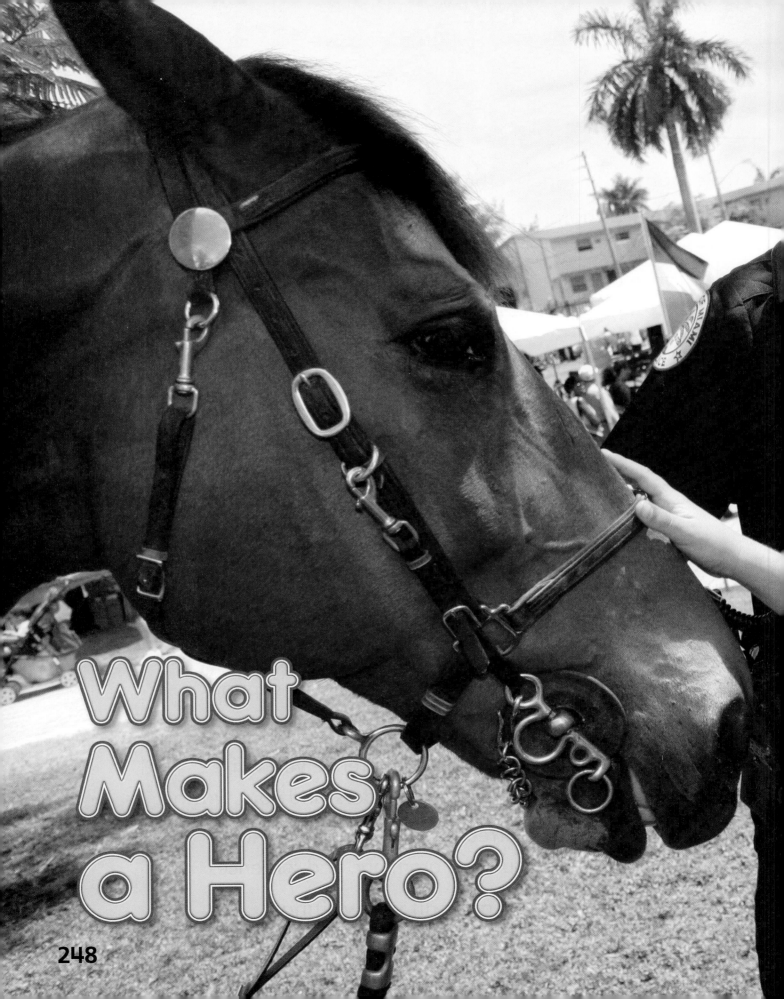

What Makes a Hero?

Talk About It

What does it mean to be a hero? Describe what a hero is like.

LOG ON ▶ **VIEW IT**

Oral Language Activities
Hero Traits
www.macmillanmh.com

ONe SLiPPery FiSH

Vocabulary

collectors
store
clever
reward
double
amount

✔ **Word Parts**

Suffixes are word parts that can be added to the end of a word to change its meaning.

collect + *ors* = *collectors*

Collectors means "people who collect."

Once upon a time, a boy named Hana lived on an island. His uncles were fishermen. One day their chief, Kula, told them to give him all the fish they catch. Kula sent his **collectors** to gather the fish. The chief's helpers took the fish to the palace to **store**. Kula promised he would keep the fish safe for his people. But soon everyone went hungry.

Hana was a **clever** boy. He was so smart that he watched the collectors carry the slippery fish. When one fell, Hana took it and brought it to Kula.

"Because you are honest and did not keep the fish for yourself, I want to give you a prize," said Kula. "How should I **reward** you?"

Hana asked the chief to repay him **double**. Hana said he wanted twice the number of fish he picked up each day. "If the **amount** is two, you give me four," said Hana. The chief agreed.

The next day Hana picked up three fish. He asked Kula for his reward. Kula was angry when he had to give up six fish, but he knew he must keep his word. Hana's family was never hungry again.

Reread for **Comprehension**

Ask Questions

Make Inferences Asking relevant questions about a story's plot can help you make an inference. Sometimes it will be about the theme, or moral lesson, of the story. Reread the story and use the chart to make inferences about the theme.

What I Read	What I Know
Inference	

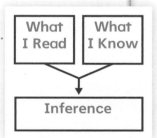

LOG ON ▶ LEARN IT Comprehension
www.macmillanmh.com

251

Comprehension

Genre
A **Folktale** is a made-up story that takes place long ago.

Ask Questions
Make Inferences
As you read, use your Inference Chart.

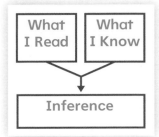

Read to Find Out
What important lesson does the raja learn from Rani?

One Grain of Rice

A MATHEMATICAL FOLKTALE

Written and Illustrated by

Demi

Long ago in India, there lived a raja who believed that he was wise and fair, as a raja should be.

The people in his province were rice farmers. The raja decreed that everyone must give nearly all of their rice to him.

"I will **store** the rice safely," the raja promised the people, "so that in time of famine, everyone will have rice to eat, and no one will go hungry."

Each year, the raja's rice **collectors** gathered nearly all of the people's rice and carried it away to the royal storehouses.

For many years, the rice grew well. The people gave nearly all of their rice to the raja, and the storehouses were always full. But the people were left with only just enough rice to get by.

Then one year the rice grew badly, and there was famine and hunger. The people had no rice to give to the raja, and they had no rice to eat.

The raja's ministers implored him, "Your Highness, let us open the royal storehouses and give the rice to the people, as you promised."

"No!" cried the raja. "How do I know how long the famine may last? I must have rice for myself. Promise or no promise, a raja must not go hungry!"

Time went on, and the people grew more and more hungry. But the raja would not give out the rice.

One day, the raja ordered a feast for himself
and his court — as, it seemed to him, a raja should
now and then, even when there is a famine.

A servant led an elephant from a royal
storehouse to the palace, carrying two full baskets
of rice.

A village girl named Rani saw that a trickle of rice was falling from one of the baskets. Quickly she jumped up and walked along beside the elephant, catching the falling rice in her skirt. She was **clever**, and she began to make a plan.

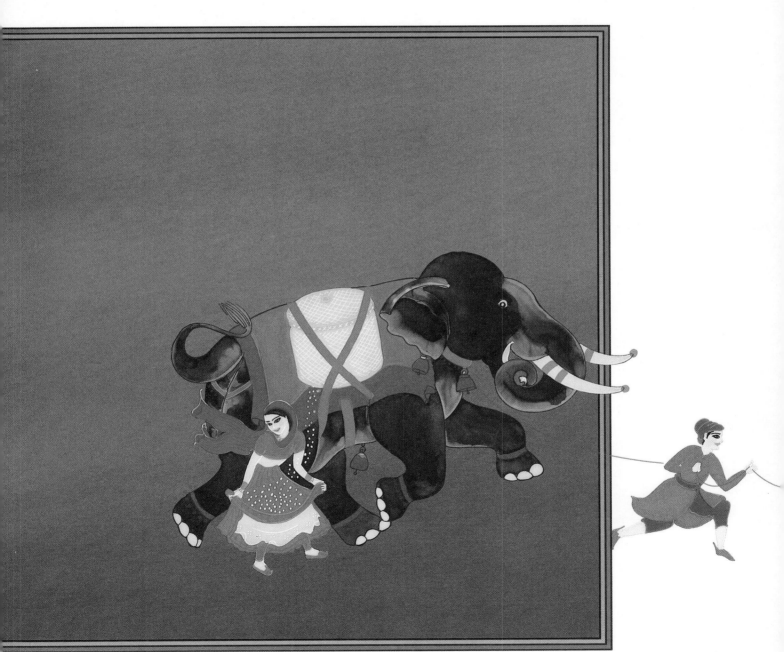

At the palace, a guard cried, "Halt, thief! Where are you going with that rice?"

"I am not a thief," Rani replied. "This rice fell from one of the baskets, and I am returning it now to the raja."

When the raja heard about Rani's good deed,
he asked his ministers to bring her before him.
"I wish to **reward** you for returning what
belongs to me," the raja said to Rani. "Ask me
for anything, and you shall have it."

"Your Highness," said Rani, "I do not deserve any reward at all. But if you wish, you may give me one grain of rice."

"Only one grain of rice?" exclaimed the raja. "Surely you will allow me to reward you more plentifully, as a raja should."

"Very well," said Rani. "If it pleases Your Highness, you may reward me in this way. Today, you will give me a single grain of rice. Then, each day for thirty days you will give me **double** the rice you gave me the day before. Thus, tomorrow you will give me two grains of rice, the next day four grains of rice, and so on for thirty days."

"This seems still to be a modest reward," said the raja. "But you shall have it."

And Rani was presented with a single grain of rice.

The next day, Rani was presented with two grains of rice.

And the following day, Rani was presented with four grains of rice.

On the ninth day, Rani was presented with two hundred and fifty-six grains of rice. She had received in all five hundred and eleven grains of rice, only enough for a small handful.

"This girl is honest, but not very clever," thought the raja. "She would have gained more rice by keeping what fell into her skirt!"

On the twelfth day, Rani received two thousand and forty-eight grains of rice, about four handfuls. On the thirteenth day, she received four thousand and ninety-six grains of rice, enough to fill a bowl.

Make Inferences
Think about Rani's reward. Make an inference about why she asked for it in this special way.

On the sixteenth day, Rani was presented with a bag containing thirty-two thousand, seven hundred and sixty-eight grains of rice. All together she had enough rice for two full bags.

"This doubling adds up to more rice than I expected!" thought the raja. "But surely her reward won't **amount** to much more."

On the twentieth day, Rani was presented with sixteen more bags filled with rice.

On the twenty-first day, she received one million, forty-eight thousand, five hundred and seventy-six grains of rice, enough to fill a basket.

On the twenty-fourth day, Rani was presented with eight million, three hundred and eighty-eight thousand, six hundred and eight grains of rice—enough to fill eight baskets, which were carried to her by eight royal deer.

On the twenty-seventh day, thirty-two
Brahma bulls were needed to deliver sixty-four
baskets of rice.

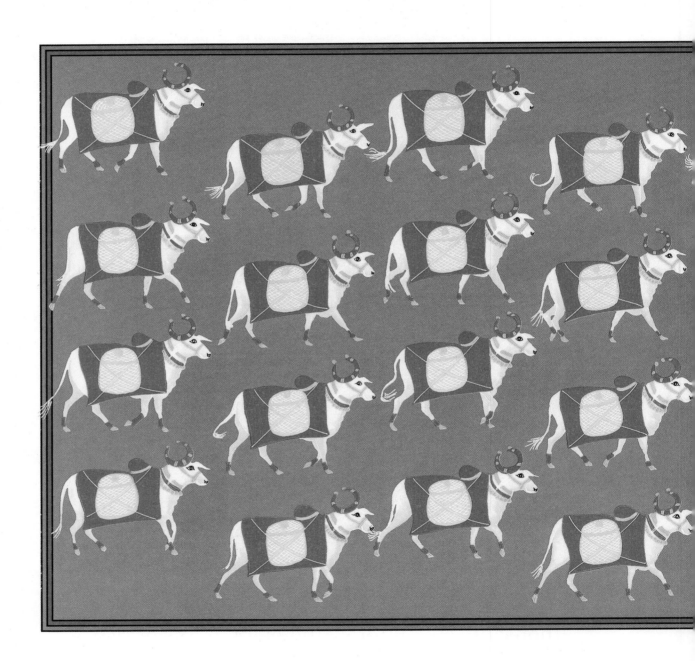

The raja was deeply troubled. "One grain of rice has grown very great indeed," he thought. "But I shall fulfill the reward to the end, as a raja should."

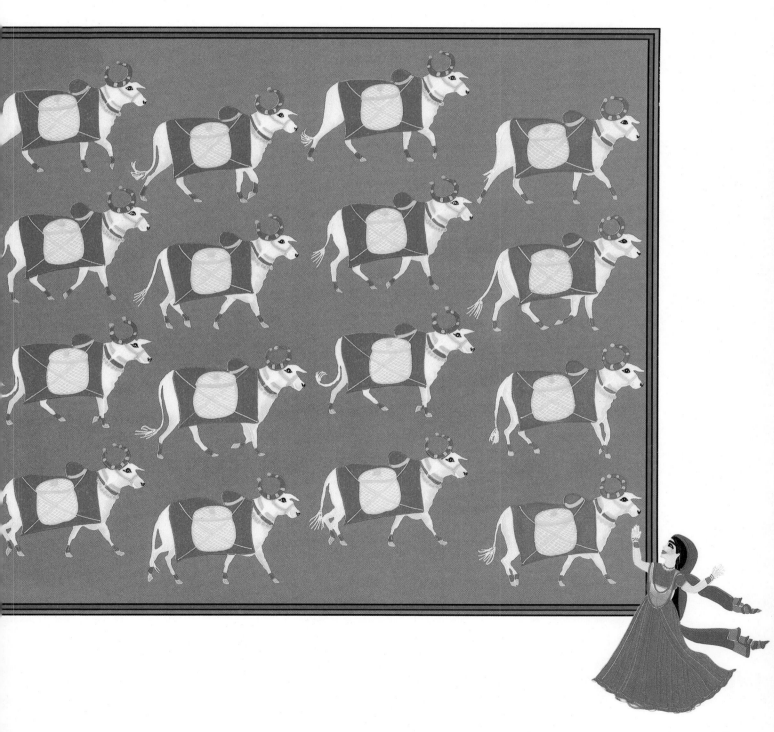

On the twenty-ninth day,
Rani was presented with
the contents of two royal
storehouses.

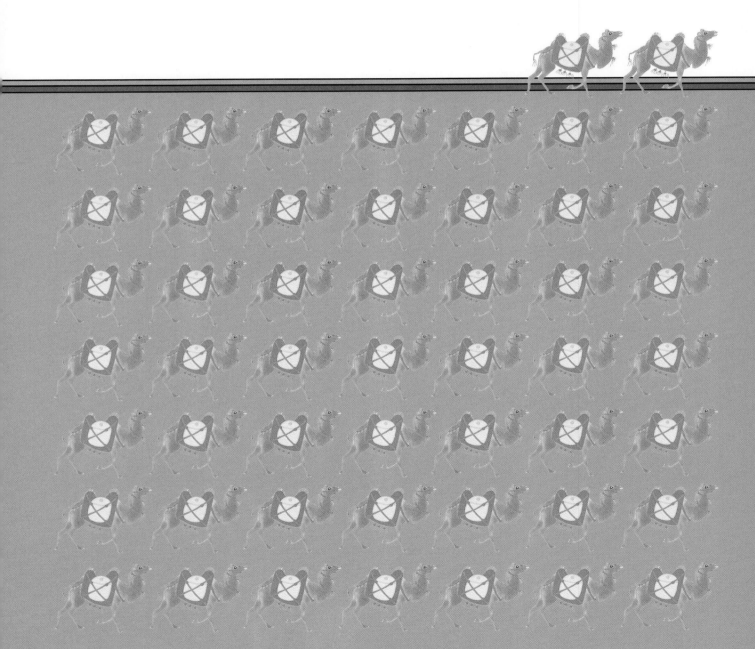

272

273

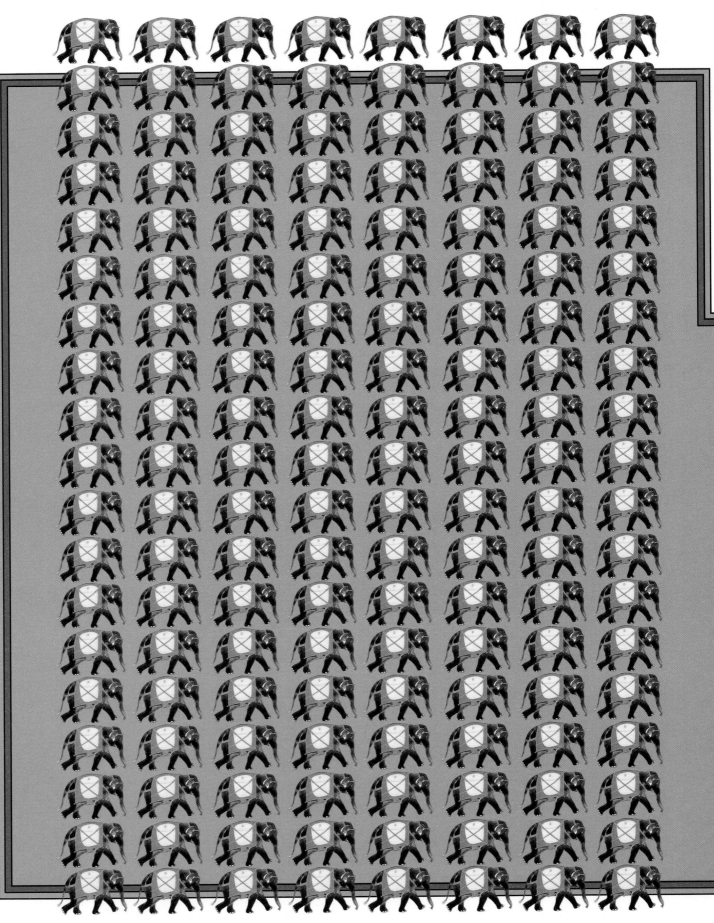

274

On the thirtieth and final day, two hundred and fifty-six elephants crossed the province, carrying the contents of the last four royal storehouses — five hundred and thirty-six million, eight hundred and seventy thousand, nine hundred and twelve grains of rice.

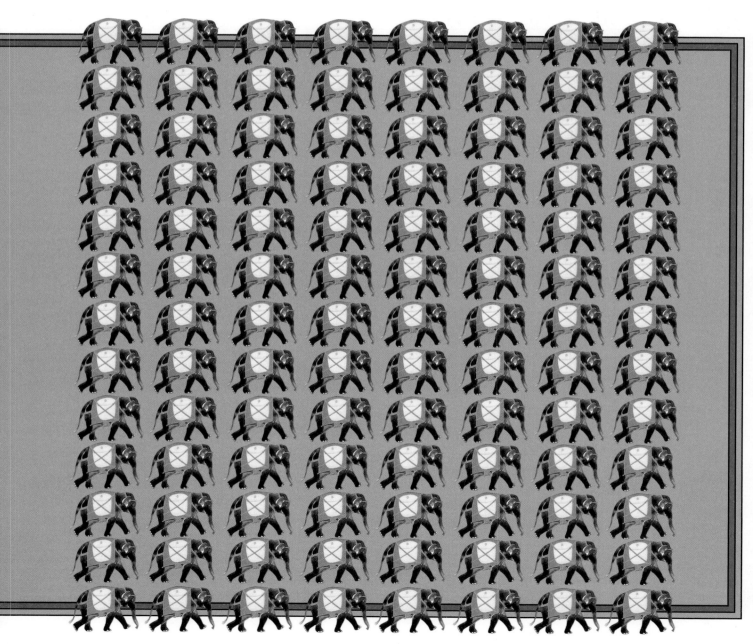

All together, Rani had received more than one billion grains of rice. The raja had no more rice to give. "And what will you do with this rice" said the raja with a sigh, "now that I have none?"

> ### ✔ Make Inferences
> Use details from the story and what you already know to make an inference about the lesson the raja learned.

"I shall give it to all the hungry people," said Rani. "And I shall leave a basket of rice for you, too, if you promise from now on to take only as much rice as you need."

"I promise," said the raja.

And for the rest of his days, the raja was truly wise and fair, as a raja should be.

TRAVEL THE WORLD WITH
Demi

𝕯emi has been an artist since she was a child. Demi's mother encouraged her to draw from a very early age. In fact Demi says that some of her earliest memories are about spending time in her mother's art studio.

Demi likes to travel around the world. She spent two years in India when she was a young adult. While she was there, Demi came to love the country's traditional artwork. Demi used that art as inspiration for the illustrations in this story.

Other books written and illustrated by Demi

Author/Illustrator Demi
www.macmillanmh.com

✓ Author's Purpose
Demi writes about places she has visited. Think of a time when you traveled to a new place. Write a paragraph about it.

✔ Comprehension Check

Retell the Story

Use the Retelling Cards to
retell the story.

Retelling Cards

Think and Compare

1. What reward does Rani ask the raja to give her? **Details**

2. How did Rani's small request grow into a large reward? Use story details to support your answer. **Plot**

3. On page 266, the raja says, "This girl is honest, but not very **clever**." Use story details and what you know to explain why the raja says this. **Make Inferences**

4. What is the theme, or lesson, of the story? What events does the author include to help explain the theme? **Make Inferences**

5. Read "One Slippery Fish" on pages 250–251. What lessons do the raja and Chief Kula learn in these two stories? **Reading/Writing Across Texts**

What I Read	What I Know

Inference

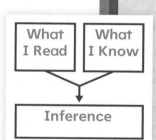

Genre

Expository text gives facts and information about a topic.

Text Feature

Headings tell what information is found in the sections of an article.

Content Vocabulary

famous

moral

summaries

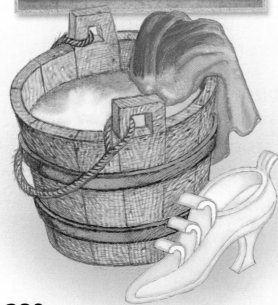

Same Story Different Culture

Children all over the world know the story of Cinderella. It is one of the most **famous** fairy tales of all time. However, people in different countries tell different versions of the story. No matter where they come from, Cinderella stories all have the same message. The **moral** is that kindness will be rewarded and cruelty will be punished. The text that follows has **summaries** of Cinderella stories from around the world.

An English Cinderella

In this tale from England, the main character is named Tattercoats instead of Cinderella. People call her Tattercoats because her clothing is so torn and ragged. In the traditional version of the story, Cinderella is mistreated by her stepmother and stepsisters. In this English version, Tattercoats lives with her grandfather, who does not treat her kindly.

In the middle of the story, Tattercoats's grandfather refuses to let Tattercoats go to the royal ball to meet the prince. Just like in the version of the story you know well, Tattercoats finds a way to go to the ball. At the party, she meets the prince. The prince falls in love and asks Tattercoats to marry him. The couple lives together happily, while Tattercoats's grandfather returns to his castle all alone.

A Chinese Cinderella

Yeh-Shen is a Cinderella story from China. Yeh-Shen's story is about 1,000 years older than the first known Cinderella story in Europe.

Like the Cinderella in the traditional story, Yeh-Shen grows up with a cruel stepmother. In this story, however, the stepmother kills Yeh-Shen's only friend, who is a fish. Yeh-Shen takes the fish's bones and buries them. The fish bones turn out to be very powerful.

When Yeh-Shen makes a wish to go to the spring festival, the fish bones give her a beautiful dress and golden slippers to wear. Unfortunately Yeh-Shen loses one of the slippers at the festival. The king finds the lost slipper and says that he wants to marry its owner.

Just like in the European version of the story, many women try on the golden slipper, but it fits only Yeh-Shen. Yeh-Shen marries the king and lives happily ever after.

Conclusion

The Cinderella character exists in many different cultures. In each story the main character may wear different clothes or go to different events. But one thing is the same in every culture. Cinderella always overcomes a difficult beginning to find a happy ending.

 Connect and Compare

1. In which section would you find information about a Cinderella story in England? **Headings**

2. Think about *One Grain of Rice*. In what ways is the English version of Cinderella like *One Grain of Rice*? How are the stories different? **Reading/Writing Across Texts**

 Social Studies Activity

Research a fairy tale from a country in Europe or Asia. Write a paragraph that compares that country's culture to your own culture. Share with your class. Speak clearly using correct language.

LOG ON ▶ **FIND OUT** **Social Studies** Fairy Tales
www.macmillanmh.com

283

Writing

✔ Vary Words

Good writers **vary words** to make their writing clear, interesting, and more exact.

I used the word <u>scampered</u> to make my writing interesting.

<u>Concerned</u> is a specific word that tells exactly how I felt.

October 10, 2---

Dear Mrs. Jimenez,

Thank you for rescuing my cousin's cat yesterday. Lenny is a curious cat. He scampered outside through an open window so he could explore our backyard. I am amazed he was brave enough to climb up to our roof! I was concerned that he would fall and get hurt. My family is so thankful that you climbed up to the roof and brought him down safely. You are a very brave neighbor!

Sincerely,
Ned Young

Your Writing Prompt

It is kind to thank people who have done something brave or heroic.

Think about someone you know who has acted bravely.

Write a letter thanking this person for doing something brave.

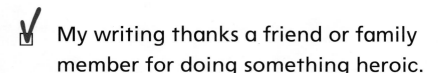

Writer's Checklist

✓ My writing thanks a friend or family member for doing something heroic.

☑ I **vary the words** that I use to make my writing more interesting and exact.

✓ I include details that give information about why I am thanking this person.

✓ I include a date, salutation, and closing.

✓ My spelling and punctuation are correct. I use possessive nouns correctly.

HEROES
from Long Ago

Talk About It

Think about things that were made in the past that people still use today.

LOG ON ▶ **VIEW IT**

Oral Language Activities
Past Heroes
www.macmillanmh.com

287

Kid Inventors Then and Now

by Kali Capria

Chester Greenwood was a fifteen-year-old who lived in the 1800s. Chester's parents **allowed** him to play outside. They let him go out even in the wintertime. Chester lived in Maine, where the winters are cold. There is lots of snow and **powerful**, strong winds. Chester would get very cold, but he would not wear a hat.

Chester decided to create something to solve his problem. He **invented** a way to keep his ears warm. He used an **instrument**, or tool, to bend wire into loops.

His grandmother then sewed fur onto them. Chester had created the first pair of earmuffs!

More than 100 years later, cold, snowy weather also gave ten-year-old K-K Gregory an idea. Snow kept getting up her coat sleeves. She looked in many stores to find an item to solve her problem. She could not find any good **products**. So K-K made a **design** for a new kind of glove. She drew and described something she called Wristies. Wristies are long gloves without fingers. They were a big hit with people living in cold places all over the world!

Above: K-K Gregory tries out her invention. Below: An ad for Chester Greenwood's earmuffs.

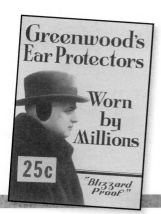

Reread for **Comprehension**

Ask Questions

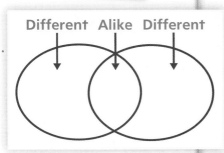

Compare and Contrast Asking relevant questions can help you compare and contrast information. To compare means to tell how things are alike. To contrast means to tell how things are different. Reread parts of the selection, and use the chart to compare and contrast these inventors.

LOG ON ▶ LEARN IT Comprehension
www.macmillanmh.com

289

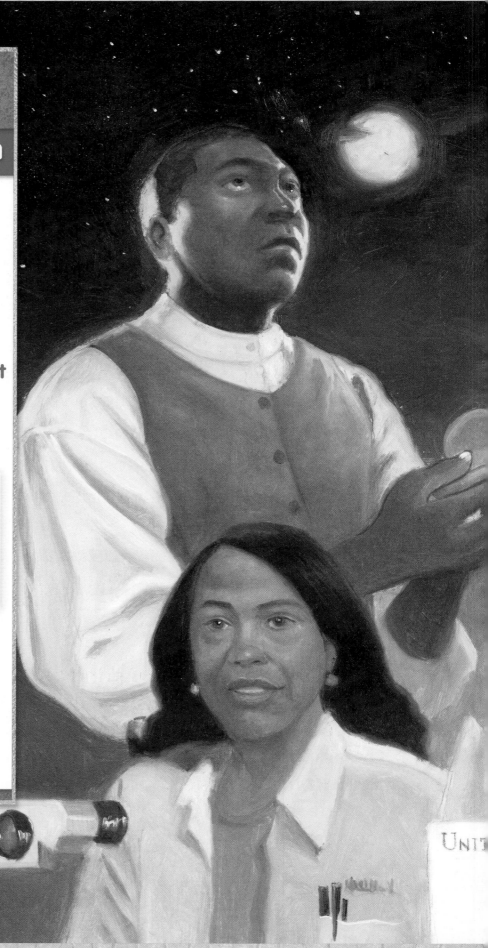

Comprehension

Genre
A **Biography** is the story of a person's life written by another person.

Ask Questions
Compare and Contrast
As you read, use the Compare and Contrast Chart.

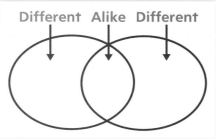

Different   Alike   Different

Read to Find Out
Set your own purpose. What do you want to find out about these inventors?

African-American
INVENTORS

by Jim Haskins
illustrated by Eric Velasquez

Award
Winning
Illustrator

ED STATES PATENT OFFICE

SARAH E GOODE OF CHICAGO ILLINOIS

CABINET-BED

291

Introduction

Inventors create new things. Their inventions solve problems or make life better in some way. Throughout our history, African Americans have **invented** many important things.

◄ John Lee Love received a patent for a pencil sharpener in 1887.

Garrett Morgan received a patent for an early type of traffic signal on November 20, 1923. ▶

◄ John Purdy and James Sadgwar patented a folding chair in 1889.

Benjamin Banneker

Benjamin Banneker was born on a farm in Maryland in 1731. At that time, Maryland was one of thirteen British colonies in North America.

Most African-American people in the colonies were enslaved, but Benjamin's parents were free. Because Benjamin was born to a free family, he could go to school.

▲ Benjamin Banneker grew up near Baltimore, Maryland, in the mid-1700s.

In the 1700s many schoolhouses were one room. ▼

Benjamin went to a local school for boys. He was so good at math that he soon knew more than his teacher. After he finished his education, Benjamin worked on the family farm.

Benjamin's life changed when he was twenty years old. He met a man who owned a pocket watch. The watch had been made in Europe. Benjamin was so interested in the watch that the man let him keep it.

Benjamin studied the watch, its parts, and the way it was made. He decided to make his own clock out of wood. It was the first clock ever made in North America.

◀ Benjamin Banneker's wooden clock worked perfectly for more than 40 years.

Benjamin used his clock to measure the movements of the stars. He used math to figure out the position of the stars, sun, moon, and planets. Years later, he wrote an almanac. An almanac is a book that lists the positions of the sun, moon, and planets for every day of the year.

Benjamin Bannaker's
PENNSYLVANIA, DELAWARE, MARY-
LAND, AND VIRGINIA
ALMANAC,
FOR THE
YEAR of our LORD 1795;
Being the Third after Leap-Year.

BANNAKER.

PHILADELPHIA:
Printed for WILLIAM GIBBONS, Cherry Street

▲ Benjamin published almanacs from 1792 to 1797.

Benjamin wrote a new almanac every year for six years. People read it to find out when the sun and moon would rise and set. They read it to find out how the weather would change each season. Many farmers used Benjamin's almanacs so they would know when to plant their crops. He was as famous for his almanacs as he was for his clock.

▲ Farming in the 1700s was done by hand. Tractors and other farm machines had not been invented yet.

Sarah E. Goode

We know quite a bit about Benjamin Banneker. We know very little about Sarah E. Goode. What we do know is that she was the first African-American woman to receive a patent for an invention.

A patent is a legal paper. It is given out by the United States government in Washington, D.C. A person who invents something can get a patent to prove that he or she was the first to have made it. No one else can say they invented that same thing.

Sarah Goode received her patent in 1885. ▼

UNITED STATES PATENT OFFICE.

SARAH E. GOODE, OF CHICAGO, ILLINOIS.

CABINET-BED.

SPECIFICATION forming part of Letters Patent No. 322,177, dated July 14, 188

Application filed November 12, 1883. (No model.)

To all whom it may concern:

Be it known that I, SARAH E. GOODE, a citizen of the United States, residing at Chicago, in the county of Cook and State of Illinois, have invented a certain new and useful Improvement in Cabinet-Beds, of which the following is a full, clear, concise, and exact description, reference being had to the accompanying drawings, forming a part of this specification.

This invention relate
tional bedsteads adapted
when not in use, so as
and made generally to
of furniture when so fo
The objects of this

ding. The folding sections B C
the stationary section A on o
thereof, so that when unfolded
section A becomes the middle
bed, while the folding sectio
respective end portions the
the stationary section A b
in the length of the bed
this well-known construc
may be obtained

Sarah Goode owned a furniture ► store in the 1880s.

▲ In the 1880s and 1890s many people moved to Chicago to find jobs.

Sarah was born in a southern state in 1850. She was born into slavery. When slavery ended, Sarah was a teenager. She was able to go to school once she was free. After she received her education, Sarah moved to Chicago, Illinois.

Sarah must have been smart and hard working. By the time she was 35 years old, she owned her own business. Sarah Goode was the owner of a furniture store.

Many African-American people were moving from southern states to northern states in the 1870s and 1880s. They moved into apartment houses. Sometimes many people slept in one room. This was because many people did not have enough money to rent their own rooms.

Sarah had the idea of making a bed that could fit in a small space. It could fold up during the day and unfold at night. She worked out a **design**. Then she made a model.

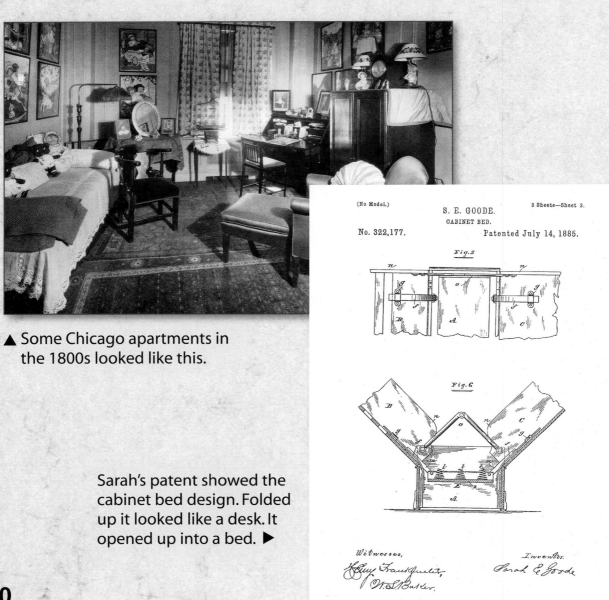

▲ Some Chicago apartments in the 1800s looked like this.

Sarah's patent showed the cabinet bed design. Folded up it looked like a desk. It opened up into a bed. ▶

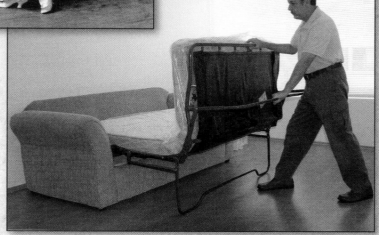

Different folding bed designs have been made over the years.

Sarah called her invention a "cabinet bed." When it was folded up, it could be used as a desk. There was even a place for keeping pens and paper.

Sarah did not want anyone else to copy her invention. She made sure of that by getting a patent.

We do not know how many cabinet beds Sarah made. We do know that her idea is still helpful for people. Folding beds are still in use today.

 Compare and Contrast
Compare Benjamin Banneker's and Sarah Goode's inventions. How did they help people? Use story details.

George Washington Carver

George Washington Carver was born in Missouri about 1861. Like Sarah E. Goode, he was born into slavery. His family was enslaved by a couple named Carver. George was raised by Mr. and Mrs. Carver.

George loved the Carver farm, with all of its plants and animals. He planted his own garden. Soon, he knew so much about plants that people called him the Plant Doctor.

▲ This is a painting of a typical farm in the 1870s.

▲ George Washington Carver at school.

▲ George graduated from college in 1894.

George wanted to go to school to learn more about plants. Slavery was over, so he was free to leave the Carver farm. It took him twenty years to get enough education and save enough money to enter college.

George went to college in Iowa. He was the first African-American student at the school. He studied farming and learned even more about plants. When he graduated, he became a teacher.

▲ George taught at his college in Alabama.

George taught at Tuskegee Institute in Alabama. It was a college for African-American people. He studied plants at the college. George told farmers that peanuts and sweet potatoes were good crops to grow. He found that he could make 118 different **products** from the sweet potato. These included soap, coffee, and glue.

▲ George told farmers which vegetables were useful crops to grow.

George learned that he could do even more with peanuts. He made over 300 different products from peanuts. Some of these were peanut butter, ice cream, paper, ink, shaving cream, and shampoo. George only received three patents for the products he invented. He believed that most of them should belong to everyone.

▲ George spent many hours working in his laboratory.

Patricia Bath, M.D.

Patricia Bath was born more than 75 years after George Washington Carver. Patricia was born in a northern state. She grew up in the New York City neighborhood of Harlem.

Like George Washington Carver, she was still young when she began to study living things. Her special interest was human diseases. After high school, she got a job helping people who studied cancer.

▲ Patricia Bath grew up in Harlem, New York, in the 1940s.

In college, Patricia studied chemistry. Then she went to medical school. She decided to study eye diseases. She wanted to find out how to remove cataracts.

Cataracts are like clouds on the lens of the eye. They make everything look cloudy. Patricia designed an **instrument** for removing cataracts. It gives off a **powerful** beam of light that breaks up the cataract. Then it can be removed.

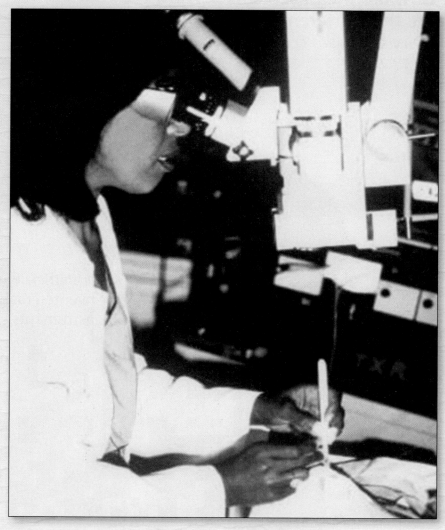

▲ Dr. Patricia Bath performing eye surgery.

In 1988 Patricia received a patent for the instrument she invented. She was the first African-American woman to get a patent for a medical invention. Since then she has invented other eye instruments. Her work has **allowed** many people to see again.

✔ **Compare and Contrast**
Compare and contrast Patricia Bath and George Washington Carver. How are their lives similar? How are they different? Use photos and story details.

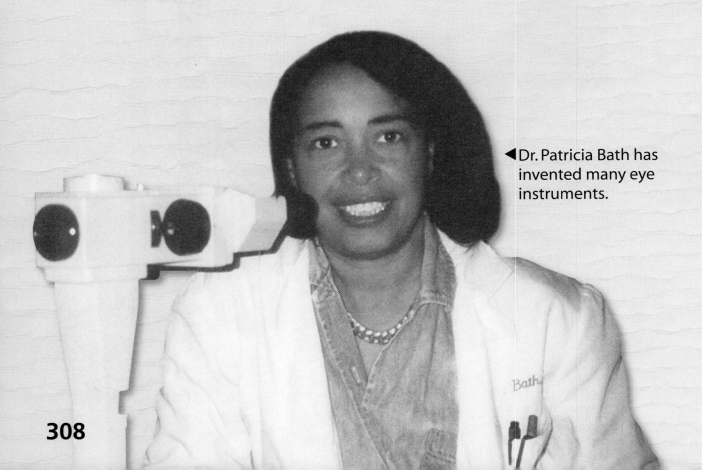

◀Dr. Patricia Bath has invented many eye instruments.

Inventors Change the World

The stories of these four inventors show how African-American inventors have helped make life better for all Americans throughout history. Benjamin Banneker helped people keep time and know the positions of the stars and planets. Sarah Goode made furniture for people to use in small homes. George Washington Carver made hundreds of products from sweet potatoes and peanuts. Dr. Patricia Bath invented a cure for one kind of blindness. The world is better because of their work.

Meet the Author

Jim Haskins was a professor and author who wrote more than 100 books. Many of his books are about African Americans and great things they have done. Some are about the history and culture of Africa.

Jim always loved to read and to learn about famous people. He once said, "I did not have any favorite childhood authors, but mostly enjoyed reading the *Encyclopaedia Britannica* and *World Book,* Volumes A through Z."

Other books written by Jim Haskins

LOG ON ▶ **FIND OUT**

Author Jim Haskins
www.macmillanmh.com

✔ Author's Purpose

Jim Haskins wanted readers to learn about certain inventors. Write a paragraph about the person you think is most interesting. Be sure to give reasons to explain why the person is interesting.

✓ Comprehension Check

Retell the Selection
Use the Retelling Cards to retell the selection.

Retelling Cards

Think and Compare

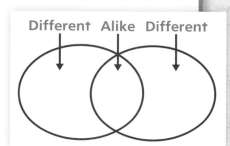

Different Alike Different

1. Where did George Washington Carver teach? **Details**

2. Use details from the selection to tell how the inventors are alike and different. **Compare and Contrast**

3. Tell how each invention is helpful. Use evidence from the text to support your answer. **Details**

4. What might the author want readers to know about the inventors in this selection? **Author's Purpose**

5. How do the **products** in *African-American Inventors* compare to those in "Kid Inventors Then and Now" on pages 288–289? **Reading/Writing Across Texts**

311

Inventors Time Line

1731 - Benjamin Banneker is born.

| 1700 | 1750 | 1800 |

1792 - Benjamin Banneker publishes an almanac. It helps predict weather for the coming year.

A time line is helpful for finding out when important **events** took place. The time line on these pages gives you **information** about some of the inventors you have read about this week. You can see when they were born and when they created their inventions.

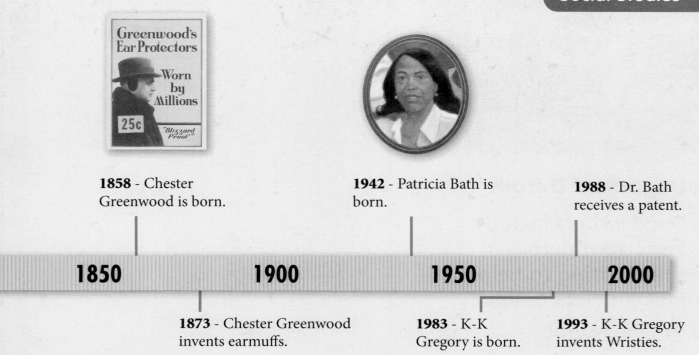

1858 - Chester Greenwood is born.

1942 - Patricia Bath is born.

1988 - Dr. Bath receives a patent.

| 1850 | 1900 | 1950 | 2000 |

1873 - Chester Greenwood invents earmuffs.

1983 - K-K Gregory is born.

1993 - K-K Gregory invents Wristies.

 Connect and Compare

1. Which was invented first, earmuffs or Wristies? How do you know? **Time Line**

2. Think about this time line and *African-American Inventors*. Choose one inventor from the selection and make a time line of his or her life. **Reading/Writing Across Texts**

 Social Studies Activity

Research another famous inventor. Make a time line that shows important events in his or her life.

LOG ON ▶ **FIND OUT** Inventors
www.macmillanmh.com

Reading and Writing Connection

This important detail tells where Grandpa Ben grew up.

This important detail is about Grandpa Ben's work.

Grandpa Ben
by Michael O.

My grandfather, Ben Rogers, is an interesting man. He was born in 1948 in California, and he has lived in ten different states. He married Grandma Lena when he was 24. They have four children.

Grandpa Ben is a scientist and an inventor. He works carefully in his lab. I always know when Grandpa Ben has a new idea. Grandpa's eyes open wide, and he speaks very quickly. Many people call him Dr. Rogers, but he is Grandpa Ben to me!

Your Writing Prompt

Inventors have created many
things to make our lives easier.

Think about a famous inventor
or an inventor you know.

Write what you know
about this person.

Writer's Checklist

✓ My writing clearly shows what I know
about the inventor.

✓ My writing sticks to the topic.

 I include **important details** about
the person I am writing about.

✓ My sentences begin in different ways.
My sentences end with the correct
punctuation. I use plurals and possessive
nouns correctly.

Review

Cause and Effect
Main Idea and
   Details
Maps
Bar Graphs
Suffixes

The Story of the Umbrella

When do you use an umbrella? On rainy days, of course! Well, not if you lived a very long time ago. People used umbrellas only on sunny days.

The word *umbrella* means shade. An umbrella would shade you from the sun. Maybe that is why an umbrella is in the shape of a tree. A tree shades you from the sun.

Umbrella History

There is another reason why umbrellas were just for sunny days. The first umbrellas were made of paper. You could never use one in the rain.

At first only kings carried umbrellas. An umbrella made you look important. Thousands of years later, women started carrying them. Women

This map shows where England is located. England is part of the country called the United Kingdom.

used their paper umbrellas as shades from the sun. Even a hat on a stick was used as an umbrella.

In England oil was rubbed on paper umbrellas. The oil made the umbrellas waterproof so that they could be used in sun or rain.

Modern Umbrellas

Umbrellas are now used around the world. They are used by both men and women. Umbrellas come in many different colors and sizes. Umbrellas keep people dry on rainy days. But an umbrella can shade you on a sunny day—if you want it to!

Rainiest Cities in the United States

Some parts of the United States receive more rainfall than others. Below is a bar graph that shows the five rainiest cities in the United States, excluding cities in Hawaii and Alaska. Each city receives many inches of rain each year. Sometimes the rain falls slowly and gently. At other times a powerful storm creates many inches of rain in just a few hours. People in these cities should always keep an umbrella handy!

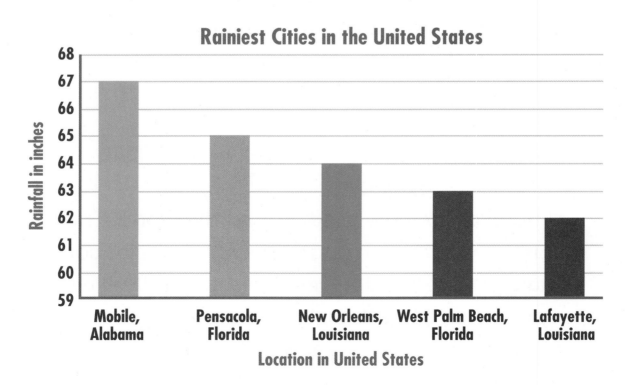

Rainiest Cities in the United States

Rainfall in inches / Location in United States

City	Rainfall (inches)
Mobile, Alabama	67
Pensacola, Florida	65
New Orleans, Louisiana	64
West Palm Beach, Florida	63
Lafayette, Louisiana	62

Bella Had a New Umbrella

by Eve Merriam

Bella had a new umbrella,
Didn't want to lose it,
So when she walked out in the rain
She didn't ever use it.
Her nose went sniff,
Her shoes went squish,
Her socks got soggy,
Her glasses got foggy,
Her pockets filled with water
And a little green froggy.
All she could speak was a weak kachoo!
But Bella's umbrella
Stayed nice and new.

Show What You Know

Comprehension

Monitor Comprehension

- Good readers use comprehension strategies such as asking relevant questions about the text. This helps you to better understand what you are reading and locate important facts in an article or a story.

- With a partner, review the biography *African-American Inventors* on page 291. Take turns rereading parts of the selection aloud and asking relevant questions about the text. Then choose two inventors from the selection and locate facts from the text to compare and contrast the two.

Writing

Composition: Biography

- Research an inventor or hero of yours. Write a biography of this person. Be sure to include important details of his or her life and what the person has done to help people.

Word Study

Phonics

Consonant Blends *sl, sp, sk, thr, spl*

- Consonant blends appear together in a word without any vowels between them. Each letter in a consonant blend has its own sound. Read the following words: *slowly, skillful, special, throw, thread, splashed,* and *split.* Identify each consonant blend.

- On a separate piece of paper, write the following sentences: *Sal got a splinter. The children threw the ball. She is a skillful writer.* Identify the word with consonant blend *thr, sk,* or *spl.* Underline each word.

Spelling

Words ending with *-ain, -ail, -ay, -ight*

- Review the following words: *train, sail, hay, sight, goes, stay, fuse, flight,* and *most.*

- Write a news story about a hero saving the day. Use each word above at least once in your story. Share your news story with a partner.

The Big Question

How do people express their ideas and emotions in creative ways?

LOG ON ▶ VIEW IT

Theme Video
Let's Create
www.macmillanmh.com

323

How do people express their ideas and emotions in creative ways?

People express their feelings and ideas in many ways. Some people use words to share their thoughts and feelings. They write plays, tell stories, keep diaries, sing, and write articles. Other people express themselves without words by playing music, painting, dancing, drawing, sewing, or making sculptures. Learning about different ways to express yourself helps you communicate your ideas to other people.

Research Activities

In this unit you will gather information. As a class we will make a list of ways people express themselves and create open-ended questions. You will choose a topic from the list and create a presentation.

Keep Track of Ideas

As you read, keep track of what you are learning about creative expression using the Three-Tab Foldable. Label the top tab "What do people create?" Label the middle tab "What tools do writers and artists use?" Label the bottom tab "Why do people create art and tell stories?"

Let's Create!

What do people create?

What tools do writers and artists use?

Why do people create art and tell stories?

FOLDABLES®
Study Organizer

Digital Learning

LOG ON ▶ **FIND OUT** www.macmillanmh.com

StudentWorks™ Plus
Interactive Student Book

- **Research Roadmap**
  Follow a step-by-step guide to complete your research project.

Online Resources

- Topic Finder and Other Research Tools
- Videos and Virtual Field Trips
- Photos and Drawings for Presentations
- Related Articles and Web Resources
- Web Site Links

People and Places

Gene Autry, Singer

Gene Autry (1907–1998) was born in Tioga, Texas. He was a country singer and actor. He created the Cowboy Code, a set of rules for cowboys.

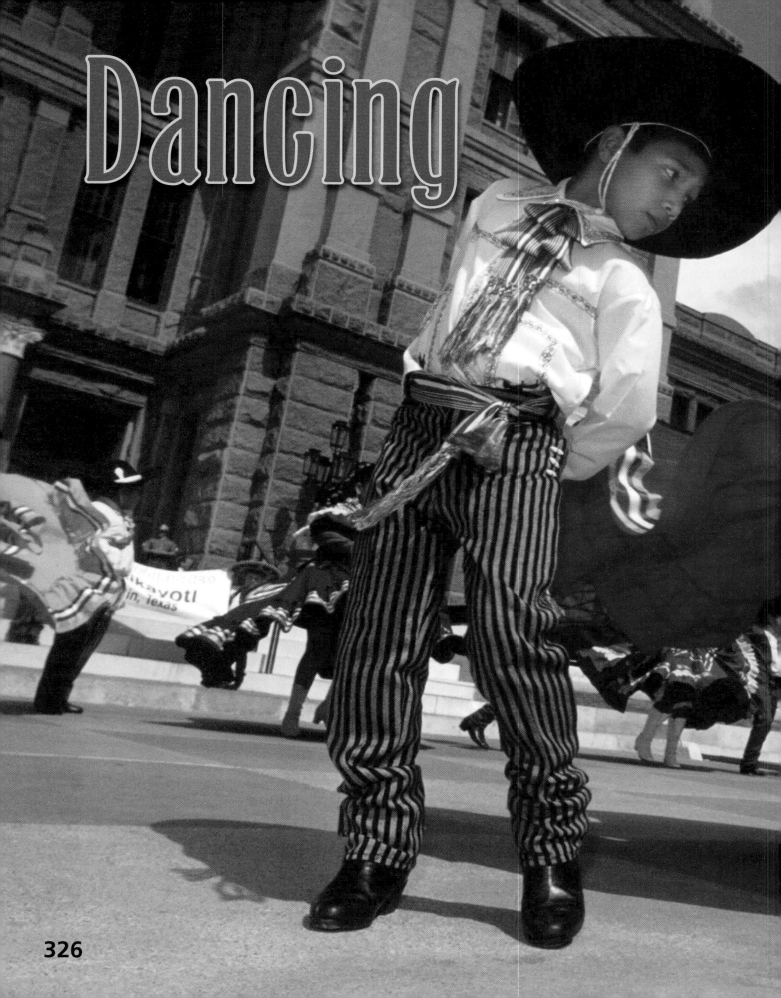

Dancing

Talk About It

Dancing is one way of expressing yourself. What kinds of dances can you perform?

LOG ON ▶ VIEW IT

Oral Language Activities
Dancing
www.macmillanmh.com

A Little Symphony

by Lani Perlin

The Fresno Prelude Symphony is a group of young people who play music. The students are children who study and learn music together. They have shows where they play their music for others. Sometimes they **perform** in front of many people.

It takes a lot of **effort** to be part of a symphony. The students work hard to do their best. They practice once a week. This helps them **remember** how to play the songs. They do not want to forget the music.

The students can play many different songs. Each song has its own **mood**. The mood is the feeling that people get when they listen to the music.

One thing is always the same, though. People leave the shows feeling glad. The people who live in Fresno are **proud** of the symphony. Many are happy to say it is the best little symphony in California!

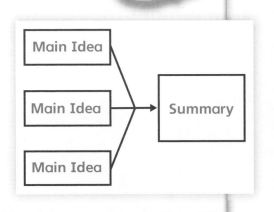

Reread for **Comprehension**

Visualize

Summarize Visualizing, or forming pictures in your mind, can help you summarize. When you summarize what you are reading, you use the main ideas of different parts of the article. Reread the article and fill out the chart to help you write a summary.

Main Idea	
Main Idea	Summary
Main Idea	

LOG ON ▶ LEARN IT Comprehension
www.macmillanmh.com

Genre
Expository text gives information and facts about a topic.

Visualize
Summarize
As you read, use the Summarize Chart.

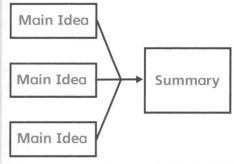

Read to Find Out
Who are the Alvin Ailey kids and what do they do?

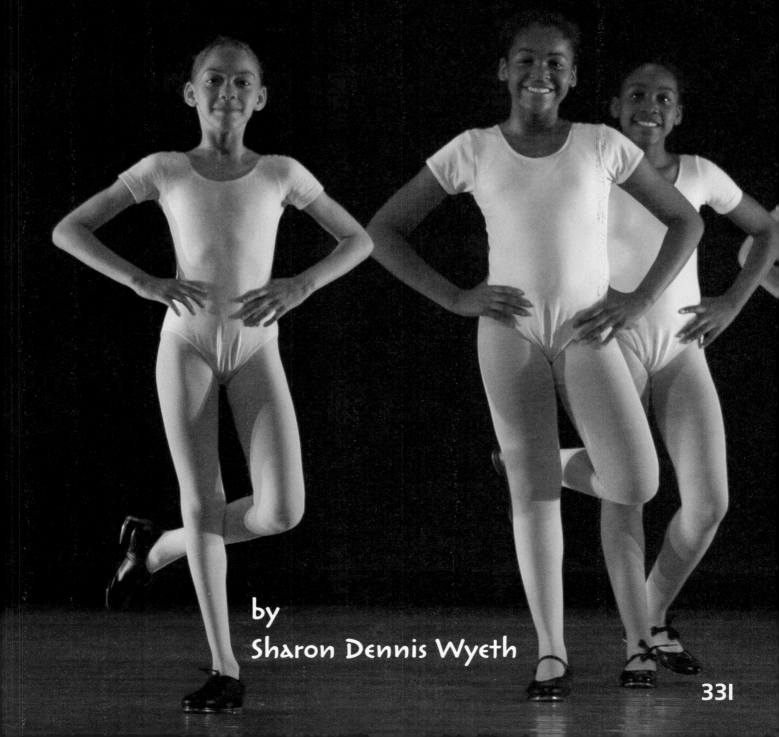

The Alvin Ailey Kids

Dancing As a Team

by
Sharon Dennis Wyeth

331

Alvin Ailey Kids

At The Alvin Ailey School in New York City, kids study dance. They take dance classes after school. They take classes on Saturday. Hundreds of students dance at the school.

Each spring the students at Ailey **perform** in front of an audience. The dancers show what they have learned during the year.

Dancing is hard work. The steps have to be done just right. That takes a lot of practice. It's also a team **effort**.

The teachers help the students learn the steps. They try to make the classes fun. The musicians also do their part. The kids have a great time while they are learning.

Summarize
Summarize what you know so far about the Ailey school. Describe the people who learn and work there.

Getting Ready in the **Spring**

J asper and Whitney attended the Ailey school in the spring of 2004. Jasper was nine years old. Whitney was ten. Jasper started to dance when he was four. When Whitney was very young, she went with her family to a ballet.

"I knew then that I wanted to dance myself," said Whitney. "Dance helps me to express myself."

Jasper, Whitney, and the other Ailey students were excited in May. Their performance was coming up. They had two more weeks to practice. Then they would perform in a real theater.

They would show their parents and friends what they had learned. First, they had more work to do to get ready for the show.

Dance Classes

The girls in Whitney's ballet class practiced their steps. Their teacher, Melanie, helped them. She wanted them to do their best.

"Arms open, girls!" Melanie told them.

Teamwork was a big part of the dance. Everyone had to do the steps at exactly the same time. "You have to dance in two ways on stage, by yourself and with a group," said Melanie.

The same girls also took tap class. The **mood** is different in tap. The music is jazzy! The shoes are noisy!

The girls tapped, stomped, and marched to the music. The dance they were going to perform was long. The students did not always **remember** all the steps. It was also hard to stay together.

"We have some more work to do," said their teacher, Vic. "From the top! 5, 6, 7, 8 smile!" Vic worked for a long time with the girls.

Jasper's favorite class was capoeira. It is a type of circle dance. To warm up, the boys stretched. They did kicks and jumps.

To do the dance, two boys went into the middle of a circle. They kicked and moved fast. All the boys took turns. They moved in and out of the circle. The boys also sang and clapped to the music.

Jasper talked excitedly about the class. "I love to dance," he said. "The thing I like best about dance is the beat!"

Capoeira

(kah-poo-air-ah)

is a dance from Brazil. Everyone forms a circle for the roda, or circle dance. They sing and clap. The dancers all have bare feet. Musicians play different instruments.

Dress Rehearsal

The day of the dress rehearsal arrived. A dress rehearsal is a final practice before the performance. It is held where the show will take place.

The students went to the theater. They thought the stage was huge. The stage manager showed them how to enter and exit the stage properly.

There were new things to get used to at the dress rehearsal. Moving on the big stage felt different. The lights were also something new.

"Watch your spacing!" said Christine, a ballet teacher. "Remember you are dancing together." The students practiced their dances one last time. The next time they performed, the teachers would not be on stage with them.

The dress rehearsal added more people to the team. "Everyone works hard for the performance," said Jasper. "Our teachers make up the dances and teach us the steps. The musicians play the music. Someone else helps with the lights. The stage manager tells everyone where and when to do their jobs. Then we do the dancing."

"The parents help out, too, by coming to watch us. For sure, my family will be there!"

Summarize
Summarize what happened during the dress rehearsal.

Performance Day

At last, the day of the performance arrived. Backstage, the dancers got ready. Then the audience took their seats.

Lights! Music! The show started! The sound of tapping feet filled the air.

The tap dancers crossed the stage together. Their feet were flying!

Ballet was next. The dancers glided across the floor with arms open. They looked as if they were dancing on air. The dance was long, but no one forgot the steps. All of their hard work had paid off.

Then the capoeira began. The dancers kicked and jumped. They clapped and sang in the roda.

When the dance was over, the dancers took a bow. The audience cheered. What a great performance!

The show was over, but the excitement did not end. Backstage, the dancers were happy. They had done a great job.

Their families gave them hugs. Their teachers were very **proud**.

"It was fun!" said Whitney.

"We did it!" said Jasper.

"We all did it together!"

Behind the Curtain with Sharon Dennis Wyeth

Sharon Dennis Wyeth knew she wanted to be a children's book writer when she was very young. Sharon says, "When I was a child, my favorite thing was reading. The library was my home away from home! Picking out a book all by myself made me feel powerful."

Sharon learned about performing when she was in high school. She sang in the chorus and acted in the school play.

Other books written by Sharon Dennis Wyeth

LOG ON ▶ FIND OUT

Author Sharon Dennis Wyeth
www.macmillanmh.com

 Author's Purpose

Sharon Dennis Wyeth wants to teach readers about performing. Think about a time when you performed. What did you do? How did you feel? Write about this experience.

✔ Comprehension Check

Retell the Selection
Use the Retelling Cards to retell the selection.

Retelling Cards

Think and Compare

1. What school do Jasper and Whitney attend? **Details**

Main Idea	
Main Idea	→ Summary
Main Idea	

2. Why does Vic tell the tap dancing class they have more work to do? Use details from the selection to help support your answer. **Draw Conclusions**

3. Use the most important ideas from the text to help summarize the selection. **Summarize**

4. The dancers put a lot of **effort** into learning their steps. What does the author want readers to learn? **Author's Purpose**

5. How are the performers in "A Little Symphony" on pages 328–329 and *Dancing As a Team* alike? How are they different? **Reading/Writing Across Texts**

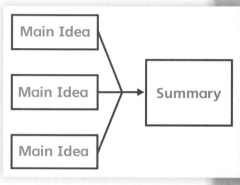

349

You'll Sing a Song and I'll Sing a Song

by Ella Jenkins

You'll sing a song
And I'll sing a song,
Then we'll sing a song together.
You'll sing a song
And I'll sing a song
In warm or wintery weather.

350

You'll play a tune
And I'll play a tune,
Then we'll play a tune together.
You'll play a tune
And I'll play a tune
In warm or wintery weather.

You'll hum a line
And I'll hum a line,
Then we'll hum a line together.
You'll hum a line
And I'll hum a line
In warm or wintery weather.

 Connect and Compare

1. What are two groups of words in these lyrics that show alliteration? **Alliteration**

2. Reread pages 332–333 in *The Alvin Ailey Kids: Dancing As a Team*. How are the dance classes like the message in these lyrics? Explain why you think this. **Reading/Writing Across Texts**

LOG ON ▶ FIND OUT   Poetry
www.macmillanmh.com

Writing

Precise Words

Writers use **precise words**, or specific words, to describe a topic to readers.

I use precise words to tell who will be in the school play.

Specific words tell what the actors will do.

Come See the Best Play Ever!

You are invited to *see* the fourth graders perform a play based on The Wonderful Wizard of Oz, written by L. Frank Baum.

You will *see* Dorothy, the Tin Man, the Cowardly Lion, and the Scarecrow *sing* and *dance* their way through Oz!

The *show* will be in the *school auditorium* on June 10 at 7:00 p.m. You'll have a great time!

Your Writing Prompt

An advertisement can make people want to
be a part of something or do something.

Think about what you could write an
advertisement for. Would you like to have
people read a book or see a show?

Write an advertisement
about this topic.

Writer's Checklist

✓ My advertisement makes people want
to do something.

✓ My writing has a main idea supported
by details.

☑ I use **precise words** and details to make
my meaning clear.

✓ My sentences start with capital letters. I
use action verbs correctly in my writing.

Folktales

Describe a folktale you know. Explain why you like it.

LOG ON ▶ VIEW IT

Oral Language Activities
Folktales
www.macmillanmh.com

Vocabulary

- medium
- stubborn
- noticed
- cozy
- arrive
- argue

Context Clues

An **idiom** is a group of words with a meaning that is different from the meanings of the words in it.

Kari will *call it a day*.

Kari will stop what she is doing and leave.

Goldilocks and the Three Bears

By Elsa Novek

Every morning the Bear family ate porridge from special bowls. Mr. Bear had a big bowl. Baby Bear had a small bowl. Mrs. Bear had a **medium** bowl. Mrs. Bear's bowl was bigger than the small bowl but smaller than the large bowl.

One morning the porridge was too hot. The bears went for a walk outside to pass the time while the porridge cooled. Mrs. Bear asked Baby Bear to close the door.

"I won't do it!" said Baby Bear.

"Do not be so **stubborn**," said Mrs. Bear. "It is not nice to do only what you want."

After the bears left, a girl named Goldilocks walked by the home. Goldilocks **noticed** the open door. She looked at it and said, "This home looks **cozy**! It is warm and comfortable. I will go inside."

Goldilocks did not stay long. It was almost time to **arrive** at school. She had to get there soon, so she decided to call it a day. Before she left, Goldilocks ate all of the porridge.

Soon the bears returned home. They saw their empty bowls and began to **argue**. "We should not fight," Mrs. Bear said, "but the next time we leave, Baby Bear must close the door."

Reread for **Comprehension**

Visualize

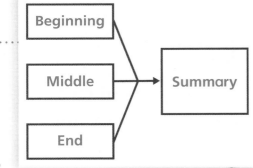

Summarize Visualizing, or forming pictures in your mind is one way to clarify what is happening in a story. Visualizing can also help you summarize. When you summarize a story, you tell only the most important ideas from the beginning, middle, and end. Reread the story and use the chart to summarize.

LOG ON ▶ LEARN IT Comprehension
www.macmillanmh.com

357

Comprehension

Genre
A **Fairytale** is a story with made-up characters and events that could not happen in real life.

Visualize
 **Summarize**
As you read, use the Summarize Chart.

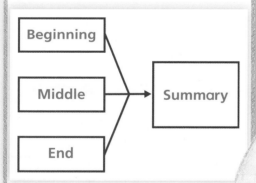

Read to Find Out
How does Abuelo entertain Emilio while they wait for his cousins?

358

Abuelo and The Three Bears

by Jerry Tello

illustrated by Ana López Escrivá

GLOSSARY

Abuelo	Grandfather
Osito	Little Bear
Frijoles	Beans
Buenos días	Good morning
¡Ay!	Oh!
Trencitas	Little Braids
Tortillas	Thin corn pancakes
Salsa	Spicy tomato and chile dip

It was a quiet Sunday. Emilio and his grandfather sat on the front porch.

"Abuelo," said Emilio, "do we have to wait much longer? When will everybody get here?"

"Your cousins will **arrive** soon," Abuelo answered, "and we'll have a fine dinner. I'll tell you a story to help pass the time."

Once there were three bears who lived in the woods—Papá Bear, Mamá Bear, and their little Osito. One Sunday morning, Papá Bear woke up as grumpy as ever. Then he smelled something good. "Mmmm, frijoles!" he said.

"Abuelo, you're joking!" laughed Emilio. "Bears don't like beans!"

"Well, all the bears I know like frijoles," said Abuelo.

Papá Bear got up and rushed down to the kitchen. "Buenos días," said Papá Bear to Mamá Bear and Osito.

Papá Bear sat down at the table and tucked a napkin under his chin. "How are the frijoles? Are they ready yet?" he asked. "Yes," answered Mamá Bear, "but they're still too hot to eat."

"I can't wait," said Papá Bear. "I'm so hungry I could eat an elephant."

"Abuelo," said Emilio, "bears don't eat elephants."

"Emilio," answered Abuelo, "you must never **argue** with a hungry bear."

Stubborn Papá Bear didn't listen to Mamá Bear's warning.

"¡Ay!" he growled, jumping out of his chair. "These beans are too hot!"

"I told you so," said Mamá Bear. "Why don't we take a walk into town while they cool?"

"All right," grumbled Papá Bear, whose mouth was still burning. So the bears left their breakfast to cool and went out.

7

Just then, in another part of the woods, a girl named Trencitas set out from her house to visit her friend, Osito. She was called Trencitas because she had long black braids.

"Abuelo," Emilio called out, "the girl in this story is called Goldilocks and she has blond hair."

"Goldilocks?" Abuelo shrugged. "In my story it was Trencitas with her long black braids who came to visit. And she was hungry, too!"

 Summarize
Use details from the story to summarize what has happened so far.

When Trencitas arrived at Osito's house, she **noticed** that the door was open. So she stepped inside and followed her nose until she came to the three bowls of beans.

First Trencitas tasted some beans from the great big bowl, but they were too hot. Then she tasted some from the **medium**-sized bowl, but they were too cold. Finally she tasted some from the little bowl, and they were just right. So she finished them all up.

Now Trencitas decided to sit in the living room and wait for the bears to return. She sat in the great big chair, but it was too hard. She sat in the medium-sized chair, but it was too soft. Then she sat in the little chair, and it was just right until… CRASH!

"Abuelo, what's Trencitas going
to do?" asked Emilio. "She broke her
friend's chair."

"Don't worry," Abuelo said. "She'll
come back later with glue and leave it
like new."

Trencitas was feeling very sleepy. She went upstairs to take a rest. First she tried the great big bed, but the blanket was scratchy. Then she tried the medium-sized bed, but it was too lumpy. Finally, she tried the little bed. It was too small, but it was so **cozy** and soft that Trencitas soon fell asleep.

When the three bears came home, Papá Bear headed straight to the kitchen to eat his frijoles.

"¡Ay!" he growled when he saw his bowl. "Somebody's been eating my beans."

"And somebody's been eating my beans," said Mamá Bear.

"And there's only one bean left in my bowl," said Osito.

Then the three bears went into the living room.

"¡Ay!" said Papá Bear when he saw that his chair had been moved. "Somebody's been sitting in my chair."

"And somebody's been sitting in my chair," said Mamá Bear.

"And my chair is all over the place!" said Osito.

The three bears climbed the stairs to check out the bedrooms. Papá Bear went first. Mamá Bear and Osito followed behind him.

"¡Ay!" said Papá Bear, when he looked in the bedroom. "Somebody's been sleeping in my bed."

"And somebody's been sleeping in my bed," said Mamá Bear.

"Look who's sleeping in my bed!" said Osito. He ran over to Trencitas and woke her up. Then they all had a good laugh.

By now it was getting late. Mamá Bear said they'd walk Trencitas home to make sure she got there safely.

Papá Bear did not like this idea. "Another walk!" he growled. "What about my frijoles?"

"There'll be beans at my house," offered Trencitas.

"I'll bet that made Papá Bear happy," said Emilio.

"You're right," said Abuelo. "Here's what happened next...."

When they all arrived at Trencitas's house, they sat down at a long table with Trencitas's parents, grandparents, uncles, aunts, and lots of cousins. They ate pork and fish and chicken and tortillas and beans and salsa so hot it brought tears to their eyes. And they laughed and they shared stories.

"So you see, Emilio," said Abuelo, "Papá Bear had to wait a long time to eat his frijoles. But, in the end, he had a wonderful meal and lots of fun, just as you will when your cousins arrive."

Summarize

How can you summarize this story? Use details from the beginning, middle, and end.

"Is that the end of the story?" Emilio asked.

"Yes," answered Abuelo, "and it's the end of your waiting, too!"

Meet the Author

Jerry Tello grew up in Los Angeles, California. Jerry's books for children reflect his Mexican and Texan family background. He writes bilingual books with text in both English and Spanish, just like *Abuelo and the Three Bears*. Jerry also spends his time working with parents and children across the country.

Other books by Jerry Tello

 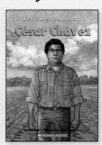

LOG ON ▶ FIND OUT

Author Jerry Tello
www.macmillanmh.com

✔ **Author's Purpose**

Jerry Tello writes stories about his own culture. Think of a story that your family likes to tell. Write about that story.

✔ Comprehension Check

Retell the Story

Use the Retelling Cards to retell the story.

Retelling Cards

Think and Compare

1. Who are Emilio and Abuelo waiting for? **Details**

2. How have Emilio's feelings changed after listening to Abuelo's story? Use details from the story to support your answer. **Character**

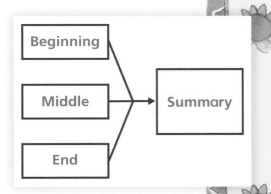

3. Use story details to summarize Trencitas's visit to the bears' house. **Summarize**

4. Why does the author describe Papá Bear and Emilio in the same way at the end of the story? **Author's Purpose**

5. Read "Goldilocks and the Three Bears" on pages 356–357. How is *Abuelo and the Three Bears* different from the Goldilocks story? How is it similar? **Reading/Writing Across Texts**

~THE~ THREE BEARS

by Mary Ann Hoberman
illustrated by Michael Emberly

People have been telling the story *Goldilocks and the Three Bears* all over the world for many years. Below are the names of three different versions of the story. The version you will read next has text that rhymes.

  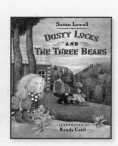

I'm Goldilocks.

    I'm Baby Bear.

What pretty fur!

    What pretty hair!

Why are you here?

    You're in my bed.

I'm in your bed?

      That's what I said.
      Why are *you* here?

I lost my way.
I found your house.
And thought I'd stay.

      And then you ate
      My porridge up
      And drank my milk
      Right from my cup.

Why, yes, I did.
You weren't there
And I was hungry,
Baby Bear.

      Well, now I'm very
      Hungry, too.

Oh, goodness me!
What shall I do?

      Where do you live?

Not very far.
A mile or two
From where we are.

I know the forest
Very well.
I'll take you home.
I'll trace your smell.

Why, Baby Bear,
You're very smart!

Get out of bed
And then we'll
start.

When I get home,
Here's what I'll do:
I'll make some porridge
Just for you.

Will you add honey
For a treat?
(That's my favorite
Thing to eat.)

I'll add some honey
If you wish.
(You can even
Lick the dish.)

Yummy yum!
I love to lick!

What comes next?

I'll let you pick.

I pick a picture book
To share.

Why, that is perfect,
Baby Bear!

The Three Bears is
The one we'll do!
You'll read to me!
I'll read to you!

 Connect and Compare

1. Which words in this selection rhyme? How do you know? **Rhyme**

2. Think about the baby bear in *Abuelo and the Three Bears*. Compare the baby bear in that story with the baby bear in this version of the story. Use details from the stories to compare the characters. **Reading/Writing Across Texts**

3. Write a poem about a fairy tale you know. Use words that rhyme in your poem. **Rhyme**

Reading and Writing Connection

I told the story events in the right order.

I put the last event at the end of the story.

My Dog Story

One Monday, a sad dog followed me home after school. He wagged his tail, but he did not look very happy. This dog kept following me for the next few days. On Friday, my dad found out that the dog had no home. Dad said my family could keep the dog. We named him Homer. I am happy we have a great new pet.

Your Writing Prompt

Stories are fun to write and share.

Think about a time when something special happened to you.

Now write a story about that event. Be sure to include a beginning, middle, and end.

Writer's Checklist

✓ My writing presents a real story.

✓ The **sequence of events** in my story is in the correct order.

☑ I include details that tell about the characters and what happens.

✓ My sentences and spelling are correct. The subjects of my sentences agree in number with the verbs.

Talk About It

How do art and music express what a person may be thinking?

LOG ON ▶ **VIEW IT**

Oral Language Activities
Art and Music
www.macmillanmh.com

ART AND MUSIC

A Chinese artist creates a bear out of ice.

People enjoy the ice slide at the Winter Carnival in Quebec, Canada.

Frozen Art

Does it seem **impossible** for a block of ice to become a work of art? Some artists make it happen. Using special tools, the sculptors make interesting figures and shapes out of ice.

Ice art is popular in many places around the world. In Harbin, China, nearly a million people attend the Ice Lantern Festival to see the ice sculptures. In Canada people go to the Winter Carnival in Quebec. Here they can stay at a hotel made entirely of ice!

So the next time it snows, imagine what beautiful artistic **treasures** you could create. Practice hard and watch your sculpture come to life. You'll see a wonderful, one-of-a kind piece of art!

LOG ON ▶ FIND OUT   Ice Art
www.macmillanmh.com

Elephant Artists

Think only people can paint pictures? Think again! In Thailand, two elephants named Boon Yang and Bird are artists. With paintbrushes clutched in their trunks, they create works of art. You might not think elephants have much **talent**, but these two are very capable artists. Their paintings sell for more than a thousand dollars each!

Boon Yang and Bird used to work with people clearing trees in forests. But the time came when their help was no longer needed. Two human artists wanted to find a **pleasant** way to keep the elephants busy. Now Boon Yang and Bird spend their time painting, which they seem to enjoy. Some of their paintings even hang in museums!

◄Trainers encourage elephant artists Boon Yang and Bird to paint.

▲ This is one of the elephant's paintings.

This exhibit shows what people from the Stone Age might have looked like.

Comprehension

Genre
Expository text gives information about real people, places, and events.

Ask Questions
Author's Purpose
When you read, you should identify the author's reason for writing the text.

Music of the Stone Age

How do we know that people made music thousands of years ago?

Today recorded music surrounds us. You can buy CDs of your favorite music. You can hear singers on the radio. You can even watch them on TV. Thousands of years from now, people will know about our music because we have made recordings of it.

Thousands of years ago, recording music was **impossible**. So how do we know that people long ago played music? Because scientists have found flutes that are 9,000 years old! The flutes were found in China, in the Yellow River Valley. Here scientists unearthed all sorts of **treasures**, including 36 flutes.

CHINA

Yellow River

Yellow River Valley

This map shows the Yellow River Valley in China, where the flutes were found.

These are some of the ancient flutes found in China. The one in the middle can still be played.

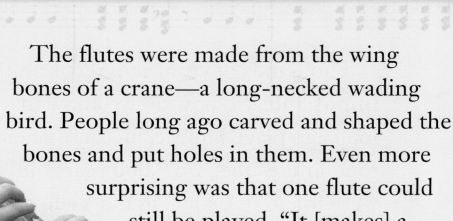

The flutes were made from the wing bones of a crane—a long-necked wading bird. People long ago carved and shaped the bones and put holes in them. Even more surprising was that one flute could still be played. "It [makes] a reedy, **pleasant** sound, a little thin, like a recorder," one scientist described.

The ancient flutes made a sound like a modern recorder.

What Is Sound?

Sound is a kind of energy that you can hear. Sound is made when something vibrates, or moves quickly back and forth. When something vibrates, it makes the air vibrate, too. Vibrating air carries the sound you hear.

Today people can enjoy recorded music as well as live music at concerts like this one.

No one knows for sure what type of music the people from the Stone Age played. Did it sound like the music of today? Did people have musical **talent** and perform concerts? Did people sing along? We can only wonder what their music might have sounded like!

✔ **Think and Compare**

1. Where did scientists find ancient flutes?

2. Use details from the text to explain how a flute makes sound.

3. What does the author want readers to learn about in the selection?

4. Why are sculptures from "Frozen Art" and flutes from "Music of the Stone Age" considered treasures?

Test Practice

Answering Questions
Sometimes the answer is on the page. Sometimes it is not. You must look for clues.

A crane lifts this Chromosaur into place at the Dallas Museum of Natural History.

The Art of Recycling

1. An artist in Mexico makes tiny furniture from bottle caps. An artist in Liberia cuts up old sandals from the trash to create a toy helicopter. People around the world make artwork and toys from trash. In some places trash is the only material that artists can afford.

2. Artists in the United States recycle, too. John Kearney is a 74-year-old artist from Illinois who recycles. He thinks junk is great for making art. He made three giant dinosaur sculptures out of chrome car bumpers he found in the trash. He called them Chromosaurs. One of them was 18 feet tall!

3. Recycling can be a lot more than just tossing trash into a bin. A work of art can be beautiful whether it's made with paint, clay, or even recycled trash.

DIRECTIONS
Decide which is the best answer to each question.

1 Some artists recycle to —

(A) get free supplies

(B) recycle old art

(C) show that art is junk

(D) make more trash

2 The Chromosaur and toy helicopter both are —

(A) children's toys

(B) made from trash

(C) from Illinois

(D) made from car parts

3 In paragraph 2, John Kearney —

(A) uses clay

(B) makes toys

(C) makes sculptures

(D) does not use trash

4 Which is the best summary of the selection?

(A) John Kearny is an artist from Illinois. He tries to recycle all of his trash.

(B) Bottle caps and old bumpers are trash. People recycle them to make money.

(C) Recycling is about more than sorting trash. Trash can be made into art.

(D) Helicopters and dinosaurs make great toys. Kids like to play with them.

Write to a Prompt

Maria wrote about a parrot that was an artist.

I wrote my ideas down first. Then I wrote the events in the order they happened.

The Painting Parrot

Grandpa and I went to the zoo to see a parrot that was supposed to be able to paint. I watched the bird smear green globs of paint on some paper. "Anybody could do that," I said to Grandpa. "Let's go see the gorillas." Suddenly the parrot started painting really fast. It squawked, and I thought it sounded like "Look!" So I looked. The parrot had the paper in its beak. On it was a picture of a green gorilla. I guess that parrot can paint! And it can talk, too!

Writing Prompt

Respond in writing to the prompt below. Review the hints below before and after you write.

Write about a time when you were surprised.

Writing Hints

- ☑ Remember to write about a time when you were surprised.
- ☑ Plan your writing by organizing your ideas.
- ☑ Include important details to support your ideas.
- ☑ Check that each sentence you write helps the reader to understand your writing.
- ☑ Use correct spelling, capitalization, punctuation, grammar, and sentences.
- ☑ Review and edit your writing.

Writing

Talk About It

Why do you like to write? What kinds of writing do you enjoy?

LOG ON ▶ **VIEW IT**

Oral Language Activities
Writing
www.macmillanmh.com

IGGY PIG SAVES THE DAY

by Kevin Tormino

It was feeding time in the barnyard. Farmer Deb fed the pigs. But then, *BRRING!* The phone rang. Deb ran inside the house to get it. The animals waited and waited. They were getting **impatient**. What was taking Deb so long to return?

"BAA, BAA," said the very angry sheep. "MOO! MOO! MOO!" said the **furious** cows, stomping their feet. They were all mad and very hungry.

The sheep and cows sent Iggy Pig to find Farmer Deb. He was a **neutral** party. Iggy did not take sides when the animals fought.

Iggy went to Farmer Deb's house. Where *was* Farmer Deb? What would make her come outside? Iggy wondered. Then he had an idea.

"HELP! HELP!" Iggy yelled. "Come right away."

Farmer Deb looked out the front door. She wondered what the **emergency** cry was for. What could be the serious problem?

"MOO! BAA!" the animals shouted together. "We **demand** that you feed us. That's an order!"

Deb ran outside and fed the animals.

Soon they were munching happily. Later, the cows sang to Iggy. "We **sincerely** thank you. We honestly mean it! MOO!"

Reread for **Comprehension**

Ask Questions

Cause and Effect Asking questions as you read is one way to clarify what is happening in a story. Asking questions can help you understand the causes and effects in a story. A cause is why something happens. An effect is what happens. Use the chart as you reread to figure out what causes the animals to get upset.

Cause	→	Effect
⬭	→	☐

LOG ON ▶ **LEARN IT** Comprehension
www.macmillanmh.com

Comprehension

Genre
Fantasy is a story that has made-up characters, settings, or other things that could not happen in real life.

Ask Questions
Cause and Effect
As you read, use your Cause and Effect Chart.

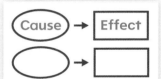

Read to Find Out
How do the cows get Farmer Brown to do what they want?

Click, Clack, Moo
Cows That Type

by Doreen Cronin

illustrated by Betsy Lewin

Farmer Brown has a problem.
His cows like to type.
All day long he hears

Click, clack, **moo**.
Click, clack, **moo**.
Clickety, clack, **moo**.

At first, he couldn't believe his ears.
Cows that type.
Impossible!

Click, clack, **moo**.
Click, clack, **moo**.
Clickety, clack, **moo**.

Then, he couldn't believe his eyes.

Dear Farmer Brown,
The barn is very cold at night.
We'd like some electric blankets.

Sincerely,
The Cows

It was bad enough the cows had
found the old typewriter in the
barn, now they wanted electric
blankets! "No way," said Farmer
Brown. "No electric blankets."

So the cows went on strike.
They left a note on the
barn door.

Sorry.
We're closed.
No milk today.

Cause and Effect
What causes the cows to stop giving milk?

"No milk today!" cried Farmer Brown. In the background, he heard the cows busy at work:

Click, clack, **moo**.
Click, clack, **moo**.
Clickety, clack, **moo**.

The next day, he got another note:

Dear Farmer Brown,
The hens are cold too.
They'd like electric
blankets.

Sincerely,
The Cows

The cows were growing impatient with the farmer. They left a new note on the barn door.

Closed.
No milk.
No eggs.

"No eggs!" cried Farmer Brown.
In the background he heard them.

Click, clack, **moo**.
Click, clack, **moo**.
Clickety, clack, **moo**.

"Cows that type. Hens on strike!
Whoever heard of such a thing?
How can I run a farm with no
milk and no eggs!" Farmer Brown
was **furious**.

Cause and Effect
What is the effect of the hens'
strike on Farmer Brown? Use
story details to help explain.

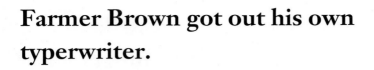

Farmer Brown got out his own typewriter.

Dear Cows and Hens:
There will be no electric blankets.
You are cows and hens.
I **demand** milk and eggs.

Sincerely,
Farmer Brown

Duck was a neutral party, so he
brought the ultimatum to the cows.

420

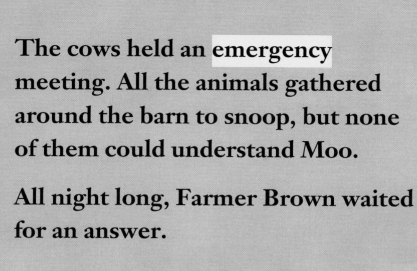

The cows held an **emergency** meeting. All the animals gathered around the barn to snoop, but none of them could understand Moo.

All night long, Farmer Brown waited for an answer.

Duck knocked on the door early
the next morning. He handed
Farmer Brown a note:

Dear Farmer Brown,
We will exchange our typewriter
for electric blankets.
Leave them outside the barn door
and we will send Duck over
with the typewriter.

Sincerely,
The Cows

Farmer Brown decided this was
a good deal.

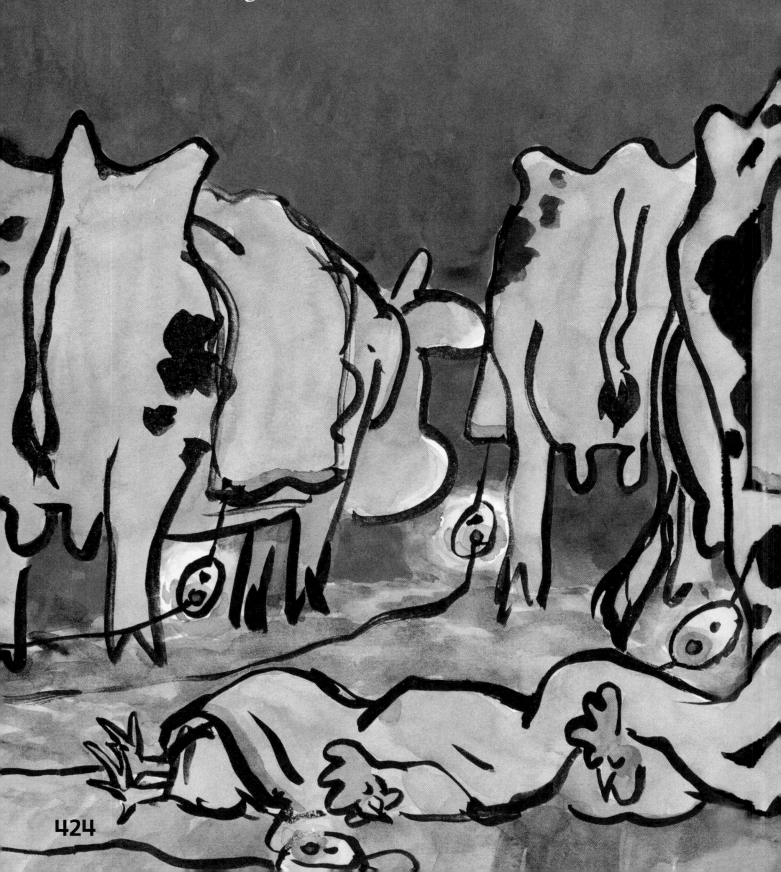

He left the blankets next to the barn
door and waited for Duck to come with
the typewriter.

The next morning he got a note:

Dear Farmer Brown,
The pond is quite boring.
We'd like a diving board.

Sincerely,
The Ducks

Click, clack, **quack**.
Click, clack, **quack**.
Clickety, clack, **quack**.

Farm Friends: Doreen and Betsy

Author **Doreen Cronin** and illustrator **Betsy Lewin** met for the first time after *Click, Clack, Moo* was published.

"I had a very, very loose picture in my head of what the animals might look like," Doreen says. "It was the publisher who decided that Betsy would be the illustrator for the book."

Betsy says that she and Doreen have become good friends and enjoy working together. "Each of us is eager for the other's comments and advice."

Other books written by Doreen Cronin and illustrated by Betsy Lewin

LOG ON ▶ FIND OUT

Author Doreen Cronin
Illustrator Betsy Lewin
www.macmillanmh.com

✔ **Author's Purpose**
Doreen Cronin and Betsy Lewin tell a story about give and take. Write about a time when you gave something up to get something else. What did you want? What did you give up?

Comprehension Check

Retell the Story

Use the Retelling Cards to retell the story.

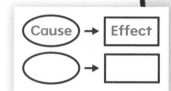

Retelling Cards

Think and Compare

1. Where do the cows find the old typewriter? **Facts**

2. What causes Farmer Brown to give the cows and hens the blankets? Use details from the story. **Cause and Effect**

3. How does Farmer Brown feel about what is happening? Use details from the story to help support your answer. **Make Inferences**

4. The cows and hens are happy. Farmer Brown then finds a note from the ducks. What does the author want readers to know? **Character**

5. How is the emergency in "Iggy Pig Saves the Day," on pages 402–403, like the one in *Click, Clack, Moo*?
Reading/Writing Across Texts

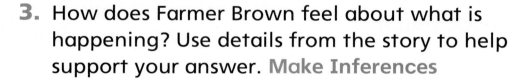

429

Early Ranching in Texas

By Linda B. Ross

More than 300 years ago, Spanish and Mexican settlers came to Texas. They brought cattle and horses with them and became ranchers.

The word *ranch* comes from the Spanish word *rancho*. These early ranchers raised cattle that were called *longhorns* because of the large size of their horns.

Texas longhorns have horns that measure 4–8 feet from tip to tip.

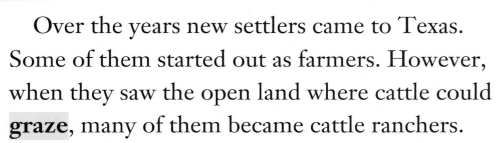

Texas cowboys came from all over
the United States and Mexico.

Over the years new settlers came to Texas.
Some of them started out as farmers. However,
when they saw the open land where cattle could
graze, many of them became cattle ranchers.

At first there were no fences separating
different ranches. The land was wide open.

By the 1860s, many ranchers hired **cowboys**
to help keep track of their cattle. The cowboys
branded, or marked, the cattle. They used the
rancher's initials or a special design. That way the
ranchers knew which cattle belonged to them.

Soon there was a big demand for Texas beef in
other parts of the United States. Ranchers were
selling their cattle in the Northeast.

Cattle Trails

Cattle drives moved north from ranches in Texas. They headed to railroads in places like Kansas and Missouri. From there the cattle went by train to the Northeast.

The drives lasted about 25 years. They ended when ranchers built fences around their property. There was no open land for cattle to roam or graze. Then railroads were built in Texas. So ranchers sent their cattle directly to market by train.

Today you can still find many ranches in Texas that raise cattle, and other animals such as horses and sheep. There are also many different kinds of farms typical to the Southwest, including vegetable, fruit, and cotton farms.

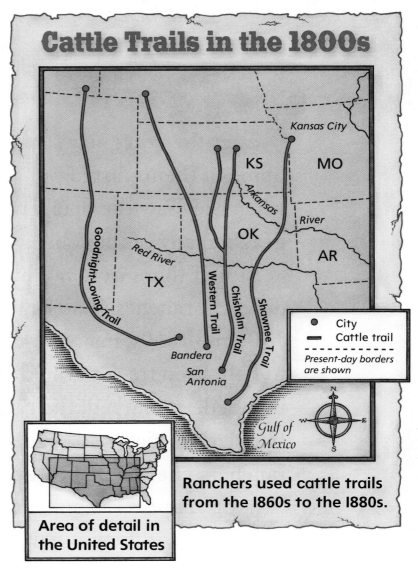

Ranchers used cattle trails from the 1860s to the 1880s.

Area of detail in the United States

432

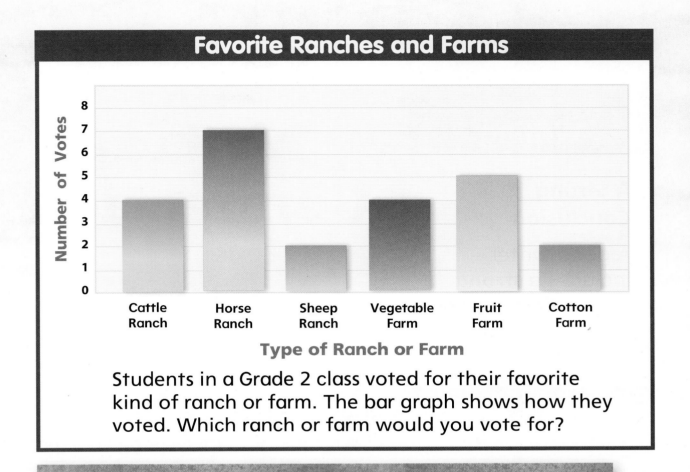

Favorite Ranches and Farms

(Bar graph — vertical axis: Number of Votes, 0 to 8; horizontal axis: Type of Ranch or Farm)

Type of Ranch or Farm	Number of Votes
Cattle Ranch	4
Horse Ranch	7
Sheep Ranch	2
Vegetable Farm	4
Fruit Farm	5
Cotton Farm	2

Students in a Grade 2 class voted for their favorite kind of ranch or farm. The bar graph shows how they voted. Which ranch or farm would you vote for?

 Connect and Compare

1. What kind of ranch received the most votes? How many votes did it get? **Bar Graphs**

2. How are the farm animals you read about in *Click, Clack, Moo* different from the animals in this article? **Reading/Writing Across Texts**

 Social Studies Activity

Research what cattle ranching is like in Texas today. Tell how it is different from long ago. Use pictures to help explain.

LOG ON ▶ FIND OUT **Science** Cattle Ranches
www.macmillanmh.com

433

Reading and Writing Connection

✓ A Strong Conclusion

A good writer includes a **strong concluding sentence** that restates the main idea.

My concluding sentence wraps up my letter.

I tell *my main idea* one last time.

12 Elm Street
Raleigh, NC 34567
December 16, 2———

Dear Mayor Tan,

Why are you increasing the speed limit on Main Street? I don't think this is safe for our town.

Speeding cars are dangerous and could hurt wild animals and pets. If a car is going too fast, it won't be able to stop in time to let an animal finish crossing the street. We have to keep animals safe. I think the speed limit should stay low so animals in our town are not in danger.

Sincerely,
Anthony P.

Your Writing Prompt

People who want to share what they think about something can write a letter to a community leader.

Think about an opinion that you have about something in your city or town.

Write your opinion in a friendly letter.

Writer's Checklist

☑ My writing is a letter that clearly presents my opinion on a topic.

☑ I restate my main idea in a **strong concluding sentence**.

☑ I include precise words to show how I feel about the topic.

☑ My punctuation and capitalization are correct. I use the verb *have* correctly.

Our Stories

Talk About It

Do you like using
words or pictures
to tell your stories?
Explain.

LOG ON ▶ **VIEW IT**

Oral Language Activities
Creating Stories
www.macmillanmh.com

437

creating

familiar

occasions

memories

imagination

glamorous

✔ Word Parts

Word **roots** can sometimes tell you the meaning of a new or unfamiliar word.

The word *imagination* comes from the Latin root *imag. Imag* means "likeness or picture."

Making Stories Happen

Illustrator Joe Cepeda

When you read a book, do you think that the illustrator and author worked together? Sometimes that happens. But **creating** books is not always like that. In fact the process of making a book might surprise you. Often the author and illustrator never even talk to each other!

438

When writing a story, the author may give ideas about pictures to the illustrator. But sometimes the story is about something **familiar** to the illustrator, something that he or she has experienced in the past.

Author Pam Muñoz Ryan

For example, *Mice and Beans* is about a party. Joe Cepeda remembered **occasions** when his family had parties. The parties were to celebrate special events. He used his **memories**, his thoughts of those past events, to draw the pictures. Illustrators also use their **imagination**. They picture in their minds how characters and settings might look.

Being an author or illustrator may seem **glamorous**. It looks so interesting and exciting, but both jobs take a lot of hard work!

Reread for **Comprehension**

Ask Questions

Draw Conclusions Asking relevant questions while reading an article and connecting it to real life can help you make decisions, or draw conclusions, about the topic. Use the chart as you reread to draw conclusions about how authors and illustrators work.

Fact	Fact

↓

Conclusion

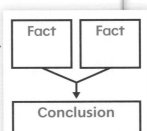

LOG ON ▶ LEARN IT Comprehension
www.macmillanmh.com

439

Genre
An **Autobiography** is a retelling of someone's life told by that person.

Ask Questions
Draw Conclusions
As you read, use the Conclusion Chart.

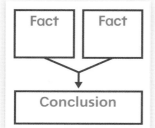

Read to Find Out
How does the author use her own life to write stories?

I moved into this house when I was four years old.

Me!

I had a lot of great friends growing up.

Stirring Up Memories

by
Pam Muñoz Ryan

Here I am with my favorite doll!

My third-grade class was very big. I am sitting in the middle and wearing a plaid dress.

441

Growing Up

I grew up in the San Joaquin (wah-keen) Valley in Bakersfield, California. This area is known for its hot, dry summers. It is often more than 100 degrees! When I was a young girl, I stayed cool by taking swimming lessons and eating ice pops. I also rode my bike to the library.

My friends and I liked to eat ice pops during the hot summers in California.

I loved the library for two important reasons. First, I could check out a pile of books and take them home with me. Second, the library was air-conditioned!

At my house, I was the oldest of three sisters. Next door to us, there lived another three girls. They were all younger than me, too. Whenever we played together, I was in charge of what we did. I was the director of the play, or the mom in a pretend family. Sometimes I was the doctor who saved their lives!

Here I am opening presents at my birthday party with my friends.

I was also the oldest of the 23 cousins in my family. When we had a family party at my grandmother's house, I was the boss again. I would say, "Let's pretend this is a circus or a school or a jungle . . ." Then I would tell everyone what they should do and say. I didn't know it at the time, but I was already **creating** stories!

I was about 17 years old at this family gathering. I'm second from the right in the back row, holding one of my baby cousins.

**This family party was at my uncle's house.
I'm sitting at the table wearing the black sweater.**

Some of my favorite **memories** are of those times at my grandmother's house. The kitchen always smelled like onions, garlic, and roasted peppers. There was often a big pot of beans on the stove. A pan of Spanish rice was cooking next to it.

When we were all together, it was crowded and noisy. Sound **familiar**? My story, *Mice and Beans*, is about a big family gathering and a grandmother who loves to cook!

Draw Conclusions
Use details from the text to help draw a conclusion about why Pam Muñoz Ryan's favorite memories are of her grandmother's house.

Finding an Idea

Readers always want to know where I get my ideas. I wish I could say that I go to an idea store and buy them. As far as I know, there is no such place.

I like to visit schools. Children always ask me where I get the ideas for my books.

Real-life people like Eleanor Roosevelt (left) and Amelia Earhart (below) sometimes inspire me to write stories.

Sometimes my ideas come from something interesting I might have read about in a book. Sometimes they come from real life, like those times at my grandmother's house. Of course, the clever mice in *Mice and Beans* didn't come from real life. They came from my **imagination**.

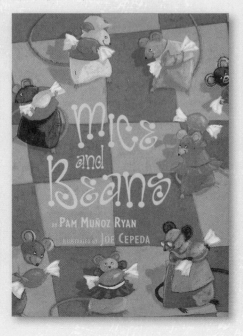

For *Mice and Beans,* I wanted to write a story about a grandmother getting ready for a big family party. I wondered what kind of party it could be.

I decided on a birthday party for the youngest grandchild. In my mind, I saw the grandmother preparing for a week. Each day, she would carefully clean her kitchen.

I thought of my grandmother, Esperanza, when I wrote *Mice and Beans*. In the photo above she is holding me when I was a baby.

Below is a picture of one of my own family parties. It is my son Tyler's birthday.

I wondered why my character was so tidy.
Was she worried about ants? Or maybe mice?
As I kept thinking, I imagined what it would be
like if she already had mice but didn't know it.
That idea made the story seem funnier to me.
Then, one thing led to another.

That's what happens when I'm writing. I start out with one idea. Then, the more I think about it, the more choices I have for the story. Sometimes I try out different ideas on paper. Then I choose the one I like best.

Now that I'm an adult, it's my turn to cook special foods for my friends and family to enjoy.

My Favorite Recipe

Salsa

2 large	tomatoes; seeded and chopped
1 to 2	chile peppers; seeded & chopped
1/3 c	chopped green onions
2 tb	chopped fresh cilantro
2 tb	lime juice
1/4 ts	salt

Combine all ingredients. Mix well and then cover. Refrigerate until serving time.

Once I've thought of an idea, it's time to start writing.

Many people think that writers look far away to find their stories. The truth is that most writers look within. They stir up memories and then sprinkle them with their imagination.

Draw Conclusions
Use text details and what you know to draw a conclusion about why Pam Muñoz Ryan says most writers look inside themselves for story ideas.

A Writer's Life

Readers often think that a writer's life is **glamorous** with fancy cars and clothes. For a very few, that might be true, but my life is much different than that.

I work at my home in California, near San Diego. I don't have to dress up to go to work. I don't take long train rides because my desk is in my house. I get up early, eat breakfast, and go straight to my office to write.

Working at home means I can walk from my breakfast table right to my office.

Sammie and Buddy keep me company when I want to work and when I want to play.

I have two friends who love to watch me work. They are my dogs, Buddy and Sammie. Almost every day, I take them for a walk, either in my neighborhood or on the beach.

For part of the year, the house is mostly quiet. My husband, Jim, and I have four children, two girls and twin boys. The girls are grown up now, but the boys are still in college. They come home during the summer. Since we live near the Pacific Ocean, there is a lot of going back and forth to the beach.

My husband, Jim, and I enjoy taking Buddy and Sammie to the beach.

Many of my favorite memories are of times spent at home.

My childhood home

Today when my children are all together in our house for family **occasions**, it is crowded and noisy. It's just like when I was a little girl. Sometimes I even cook rice and beans! During these times, we're creating new memories. Maybe someday they'll give me the idea for another story!

Stirring Up Ideas with Pam Muñoz Ryan

Pam Muñoz Ryan likes to visit classrooms. Children often ask her how to become a writer. "If you want to be a writer, first become a reader," Pam says. "Daydream every day and pretend often. That's where ideas live—in your imagination. If you think of a story, write it down and save it. Someday, it might be the seed that grows into something magnificent."

Other books written by Pam Muñoz Ryan

Author Pam Muñoz Ryan
www.macmillanmh.com

Author's Purpose

Pam explains what she did during the summer when she was a girl. What do you like to do in the summer? Write a paragraph about your summers.

 ## Comprehension Check

Retell the Selection
Use the Retelling Cards to retell
the selection.

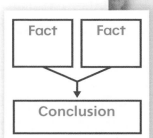

Retelling Cards

Think and Compare

1. Where did the author grow up?
   Details

Fact	Fact

↓

Conclusion

2. How did being the oldest of 23
   cousins help Pam to become a writer?
   Cause and Effect

3. Use details from the text and what you know to
   draw a conclusion about why this selection is
   called *Stirring Up Memories*. **Draw Conclusions**

4. The author includes different photos of her life.
   What do you think she wants readers to know?
   Author's Purpose

5. Read "Making Stories
   Happen" on pages
   438–439. How is Joe
   Cepeda's way of
   working like Pam's
   way? **Reading/Writing
   Across Texts**

BRUSH DANCE

by Robin Bernard

A dot,
    a blot,
        a smidge,
            a smear.
and just a little squiggle here...
A dab,
    a dash,
        a splish,
            a splat.
that's how Patrick paints a cat!

CRAYONS

by Marchette Chute

I've colored a picture with crayons.

I'm not very pleased with the sun.

I'd like it much stronger and brighter.

And more like the actual one.

I've tried with a crayon that's yellow.

I've tried with a crayon that's red.

But none of it looks like the sunlight

I carry around in my head.

✔ Connect and Compare

1. Which words in the poem "Brush Dance" are an example of alliteration? **Alliteration**

2. Think about the speaker in the poem "Crayons" and Pam Muñoz Ryan in *Stirring Up Memories*. How are they alike? **Reading/Writing Across Texts**

3. Rhyme, rhythm, and repetition help create images in poetry. Write a poem about art. Use words that rhyme or create a rhythm.

Writing

✓ **Precise Words**

Good writers use **precise words** to express their emotions and voice.

Precise words can describe my ideas.

I use precise words to show emotion.

Tea Party

by Brittany H.

A rainy Sunday, what should we do?
Mom said, "I've got an idea for you.
We'll make fancy snacks and iced tea.
I'll serve you, and you serve me!"
What a wonderful thing to do,
On a gloomy Sunday for just us two.

Your Writing Prompt

A poem can be about any topic.

Think about something you
like to do with your family.

Now, write a poem about
that activity. Your poem should
have a rhythm.

Writer's Checklist

✓ My writing is clearly a poem that describes
an activity with a family member.

✓ My poem includes a main idea and details.

☑ I use **precise words** to express my emotions
and let my voice as a writer come through.

✓ My punctuation is correct. My poem has
rhythm. I combine sentences correctly.

The WIN

Erica's twisted ankle hurt. But not as much as the thought of losing the playoff game. "How can we win now?" Erica frowned as the coach helped her limp off the basketball court.

Erica wanted the Hoopers to win, but she was the best player on the team. Everyone knew this. If they won this game, everyone in the league would know she was the best, too! And Erica wanted everyone to know. But she could not argue with the pain in her ankle.

Erica watched from the bench. Everyone on the team looked discouraged. Their faces were sad. No one thought they could win without her. It was as if a big sneaker had stepped on their hopes of winning the playoff game.

But Erica saw something else from the bench. The Hoopers were good, even without her. They could win the playoff game if they believed they could.

Erica began to cheer. "Go Hoopers! You are the best!" Everyone began to smile again. They began to win. And Erica understood that being the best meant more than just scoring points. The win for the Hoopers was a win for every member of the team.

MAKE A PIÑATA

Have you seen a piñata? A piñata is a container filled with treats. You and your friends can make a piñata.

First, make a job chart to show who will get what is needed.

WHAT YOU NEED	WHO WILL GET IT
a large balloon	Carlos
string	Jan
strips of newspaper	Kia
flour	Tanya
scissors	Sean
tape	Pedro
small, wrapped treats	Sam
colored tissue paper	Maria
glue	Marisa

MAKE THE SHAPE

Then blow up a balloon and knot it. Tie a string to the knot.

MAKE THE SHELL

Next, dip newspaper strips into the flour glue. Put the strips onto the balloon one at a time. Overlap them to cover the balloon. Let the strips dry. Repeat this step three times.

ADD TREATS

Have an adult make a hole at the top of the piñata. Pop the balloon and then fill the piñata with treats. Tape the hole closed.

DECORATE IT

Next, glue or tape tissue paper onto the piñata to decorate it. Cover all the newspaper.

BREAK IT

Have an adult help you hang the piñata in an open space. Finally you and your friends can try to break it with a stick to get the treats!

Adults and children use piñatas during celebrations.

Comprehension

Monitor Comprehension

- Good readers monitor comprehension by using strategies such as asking relevant questions and locating facts about the text. These strategies can help you better understand what you are reading.

- Review the autobiography *Stirring Up Memories* on pages 440–455. Reread parts of the text and locate facts or details about the stories Pam Muñoz Ryan has written. Ask relevant questions such as, Where did the author's ideas come from? Discuss with a partner.

Writing

Write an Advertisement

- **Persuasive Writing** Think of a favorite play or musical. Now write an advertisement for it. Add a date, time, and place. Tell about who is performing or an exciting part of the show. Include information to persuade people to see the performance.

Word Study

Phonics

r-Controlled Words

- *r*-Controlled words are words in which the *r* that comes after the vowel changes the sound of the vowel. Say the following words: *perfect, pretty, ear, corner, inside, hurt, heavy.* Identify which words are *r*-controlled words.

Spelling

Words with *r*-Controlled Vowels

- Review the following words: *turn, stir, fort, circus, offer, verb, silver, north, market.* On a separate piece of paper, list words you know with the same spelling patterns.

Vocabulary

Vocabulary

Synonyms and Antonyms

- Think of **synonyms** for the following words: start, hurry, market, offer, effort, occur
- Think of **antonyms** for the following words: perfect, inside, heavy, north, stormy
- Use a dictionary if you need to. Then use two synonyms and two antonyms in sentences.

Glossary
What Is a Glossary?

A glossary can help you find the **meanings** of words. If you see a word that you don't know, try to find it in the glossary. The words are in **alphabetical order**. **Guide words** at the top of each page tell you the first and last words on the page.

A **definition** is given for each word. An **example** shows the word used in a sentence. Each word is divided into **syllables**. Finally, the **part of speech** is given.

forest

relatives

468

Guide Words

First word on the page   Last word on the page

Sample Entry

Definition

Main entry — **celebrate**   To show that something is important in a special way. *Americans* ***celebrate*** *the Fourth of July by marching in parades.*

Example sentence

Syllable division — **cel•e•brate** *verb.* — Part of speech

habitat

469

Aa

advice An idea about how to solve a problem or how to act at a certain time. *My teacher gave me **advice** on how to study math.* **ad·vice** *noun.*

agriculture The business of raising animals and farming. *Farmers study **agriculture** to learn how to run successful farms.* **ag·ri·cul·ture** *noun.*

allowed Let someone do something. *David **allowed** Jen to use his camera.* **al·lowed** *verb.* Past tense of **allow.**

amount A number or quantity that tells how much there is of something. *The tag showed the **amount** of bagels in the bag.* **a·mount** *noun.*

argue To give one's opinion about something. *Santos will **argue** with his parents for a later bedtime.* **ar·gue** *verb.*

arrive To reach a place. *My parents **arrive** home after work each day.* **ar·rive** *verb.*

Cc

carefully With care. *After checking the paragraph **carefully**, I found two mistakes.* **care·ful·ly** *adverb.*

cattle Domestic four-footed animals held as property or for use on a farm or ranch. *Dairy **cattle** are raised to give milk.* **cat·tle** *noun.*

celebrate   To show that something is important in a special way. *Americans **celebrate** the Fourth of July by marching in parades.*
cel·e·brate *verb.*

clever   Showing intelligence or skill. *The **clever** dog performs many different tricks.*
clev·er *adjective.*

climate   The usual weather conditions of a place or region throughout the year. *The desert's **climate** is much warmer than the tundra's climate.*
cli·mate *noun.*

collection   A group of things gathered together. *The museum has the world's largest **collection** of dinosaur fossils.*
col·lec·tion *noun.*

collectors   People who gather or bring things together. *The baseball card **collectors** are looking for new cards to add to their collections.*
col·lect·ors *plural noun.* Plural of **collector**.

commotion   A noisy uproar or disorder. *There was a **commotion** when a bird flew into our classroom window.*
com·mo·tion *noun.*

company   A friend or friends. *I like to be surrounded by **company**.*
com·pa·ny *noun.*

concern Serious interest. *We were full of concern for our teacher who was out sick for a whole week.*

con·cern *noun.*

countries Areas of land and the people who live there. *The countries of Canada and the United States are part of North America.*

coun·tries *plural noun.* Plural of **country**.

cowboys Those who tend cattle or horses. *The cowboys rounded up the cattle.*

cow·boys *plural noun.* Plural of **cowboy**.

cozy Warm, comfortable, and snug. *I love to sit in my aunt's cozy kitchen.*

co·zy *adjective.*

creating Causing something to be or happen. *The children were creating new paintings during art class.*

cre·at·ing *verb.* Inflected form of **create**.

crops Plants grown and gathered to be used for food or sold to earn money. *We had huge crops of lettuce this year.*

crops *plural noun.* Plural of **crop**.

cuddle   To hold close in one's arms. *I like to **cuddle** my pet rabbit.*
cud·dle *verb.*

cultures   The arts, beliefs, and customs that make up a way of life for a group of people. *I am studying the **cultures** of China and India.*
cul·tures *plural noun.* Plural of **culture**.

Dd

data   Facts and information. *The scientist collects **data**.*
data *noun.*

deaf   Not able to hear or hear well. *Ralph uses sign language to speak to his **deaf** mother.*
deaf *adjective.*

delighted   Very pleased or happy. *The child was **delighted** when she saw her presents.*
de·ligh·ted *adjective.*

473

demand To ask for with force. *The customer will **demand** his money back for the broken television.*
de·mand *verb.*

democracy A government that is run by the people who live under it. *The United States is a **democracy**.*
dem·o·cra·cy *noun.*

design A drawing or outline used as a guide or pattern. *The architect's **design** for the museum was beautiful.*
de·sign *noun.*

different Not the same as something else. *The teammates all had **different** numbers on their uniforms.*
dif·fer·ent *adjective.*

double Twice as many or as much. *Two dollars is **double** one dollar.*
dou·ble *adjective.*

Ee

effort Hard work. *Climbing the five flights of stairs took much **effort**.*
ef·fort *noun.*

emergency Having to do with something important or dangerous that needs fast action. *Use the **emergency** exit at the back of the theater in case of fire.*
e·mer·gen·cy *adjective.*

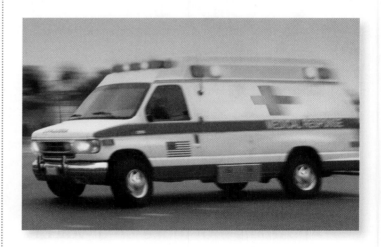

enjoyed   Got joy or pleasure from; was happy with. *My family enjoyed last year's ski trip.*
en·joyed *verb.* Past tense of **enjoy**.

events   Things that happen, especially things that are important to people. *I like to read about current events in the newspaper.*
e·vents *plural noun.* Plural of **event**.

excited   Made very happy about something. *The goalie's great play excited the fans.*
ex·cit·ed *verb.* Past tense of **excite**.

exclaimed   Spoke or shouted suddenly with strong feelings. *"I just won the game," Christopher exclaimed.*
ex·claimed *verb.* Past tense of **exclaim**.

Ff

familiar   Known because of having been heard or seen before. *The actor on television looked familiar.*
fa·mil·iar *adjective.*

favorite   A person or thing liked best. *Action movies are my favorite.*
fa·vor·ite *noun.*

figure   A form, outline, or shape. *Each figure on the shelf is part of Mom's collection of bells.*
fig·ure *noun.*

furious   Very angry. *When I forgot to do my chores, Mom was furious with me.*
fu·ri·ous *adjective.*

Gg

glamorous   Interesting, exciting, and charming. *The actor went to many **glamorous** parties.*
glam·or·ous *adjective.*

goal   Something that someone wants and tries to get or become. *Henry's **goal** is to grow up and be a teacher.*
goal *noun.*

government   A group of people in charge of ruling a country or other place. *Our **government** helps make laws.*
gov·ern·ment *noun.*

graze   To feed on growing grass. *The cattle would **graze** in the field.*
graze *verb.*

groan   To make a sad sound when you are unhappy, annoyed, or in pain. *I **groan** every time I do push-ups.*
groan *verb.*

Hh

habitat   The place where a plant or an animal lives. *The alligator's **habitat** is a swamp.*
hab·i·tat *noun.*

harvest   The gathering of a crop. *Farmers **harvest** the corn crops every fall.*
har·vest *verb.*

Ii

imagination   Pictures in a person's mind that are not real. *Ernesto used his **imagination** to create a new ending to the story.*
i·mag·i·na·tion *noun.*

immigrants   People who come to live in a country in which they were not born. *My family were immigrants to the United States from Haiti.*
im·mi·grants *plural noun.* Plural of **immigrant**.

impatient   Not able to put up with a delay or a problem calmly and without anger. *The editor became impatient when the book wasn't finished.*
im·pa·tient *adjective.*

impossible   Not able to happen or be done. *The snowstorm made it impossible to get to school today.*
im·pos·si·ble *adjective.*

independence   Freedom. *During the Revolutionary War, America won its independence from England.*
in·de·pen·dence *noun.*

information   Knowledge about something. *Where can I get information about crocodiles?*
in·for·ma·tion *noun.*

instrument   **1.** A tool that helps a person do something. *The dentist used an instrument to scrape my teeth.* **2.** Something used to make music. *Which musical instrument do you play?*
in·stru·ment *noun.*

invent   To make or think of something for the first time. *It took Thomas Edison a long time to invent the lightbulb.*
in·vent *verb.*

irrigate   To supply water by artificial means. *The farmers needed to irrigate the crops.*
ir·ri·gate *verb.*

Kk

knowledge   Having information about something. *I have knowledge about plants.*
know·ledge *noun.*

Ll

landmark   An important building or place. *The White House is a famous landmark.*
land·mark *noun.*

league   A group of people who share the same interest or enjoy the same activity. *Both of those baseball teams belong to the same league.*
league *noun.*

Mm

machines   Devices that do particular jobs. *Machines help us with everyday jobs.*
ma·chines *noun.* Plural of **machine**.

memories   Persons or things remembered from the past. *My favorite memories from camp are playing soccer and swimming.*
mem·o·ries *plural noun.* Plural of **memory**.

mood   The way that a person feels at a certain time. *I am in a good mood when I ride my bike.*
mood *noun.*

moral   The lesson taught by a story. *The moral of the fairy tale is to be kind to strangers.*
mor·al *noun.*

Nn

neutral   Not supporting either side in an argument or a war. *A neutral country does not take sides during a war.*
neu·tral *adjective.*

noticed   Saw or became aware of something. *I noticed a funny smell in the new car.*
no·ticed *verb.* Past tense of **notice**.

Oo

occasions   Important or special events. *Holidays are important occasions for my family.*
oc·ca·sions *plural noun.* Plural of **occasion**.

Pp

patient   Being able to put up with problems or delays without getting angry or upset. *The people in line were patient even though they had waited an hour.*
pa·tient *adjective.*

perform   To sing or act, often for others. *The marching band will perform at the halftime show.*
per·form *verb.*

pleasant   In a nice or friendly way. *The cab driver was pleasant to all his riders.*
pleas·ant *adjective.*

powerful   Having great power and importance. *The president is a powerful member of government.*
pow·er·ful *adjective.*

practiced   Did something again and again until it was done well. *To learn the flute, I practiced every day.*
prac·ticed *verb.* Past tense of **practice**.

479

predict   To use what you know to tell what will happen. *Scientists try to **predict** when an earthquake will happen.*
pre·dict *verb.*

products   Things that are made or created. *The cans of food you buy in stores are **products**.*
prod·ucts *plural noun.* Plural of **product**.

proud   Having a good feeling about something that you or someone else did. *I am **proud** of the painting I made.*
proud *adjective.*

Rr

rattled   Made or caused short, sharp sounds. *The windows **rattled** from the wind.*
rat·tled *verb.* Past tense of **rattle**.

record   To put information in writing. *Scientists **record** facts that they learn.*
rec·ord *verb.*

relatives   People who are part of a family. *My aunts, uncles, and cousins are some of my **relatives**.*
rel·a·tives *plural noun.* Plural of **relative**.

remember   To think of something again; to not forget. *I haven't ridden a bike for ten years, but I **remember** how.*
re·mem·ber *verb.*

respected   Looked up to someone. *We **respected** our teachers.*
re·spec·ted *verb.* Past tense of **respect**.

reward Something that a person gets for doing something good, brave, or useful. *The police officer received a **reward** for finding the lost child.*
re·ward *noun.*

Ss

settled Made a home in a place. *We **settled** in a large city when we moved to this country.*
set·tled *verb.* Past tense of **settle.**

share To give some of what one person has to someone else. *Edgar will **share** his brownie with me.*
share *verb.*

shivering Shaking or trembling from cold or fear. *We were **shivering** from the cold air.*
shiv·er·ing *verb.*

signing Showing words and letters with your hands and fingers. *Some people use **signing** to speak to one another.*
sign·ing *noun.*

sincerely Done in an honest and true way. *I would like to thank you **sincerely** for your help.*
sin·cere·ly *adverb.*

state One of the units of a nation. *Texas is a **state.***
state *noun.*

store   To put things away until they are needed. *I store my paints in my bedroom until it is time to go to art class.*
store *verb.*

stubborn   Not willing to give in or change. *The stubborn child would not eat cabbage.*
stub·born *adjective.*

summaries   Short statements that give the main ideas of stories or articles. *I write story summaries for all my book reports.*
sum·ma·ries *plural noun.* Plural of **summary**.

symbol   Something that represents something else. *The American flag is a symbol that represents the United States of America.*
sym·bol *noun.*

Tt

talent   A natural ability or skill. *Clara has a talent for drawing realistic pictures.*
tal·ent *noun.*

tangle   A confused or complicated situation. *The girl caused a tangle when she invited all but one friend to the party.*
tan·gle *noun.*

thinning   Becoming thin; decreasing in number. *Grandpa's hair is thinning.*
thin·ning *adjective.*

treasures   Money, jewels, or things that are worth a lot or have meaning. *Scientists discovered treasures in the ancient tomb.*
treas·ures *plural noun.* Plural of **treasure**.

Vv

vendors   People who sell things. *The fruit **vendors** were selling apples, bananas, and oranges.* **ven·dors** *plural noun.* Plural of **vendor**.

volunteers   People who offer to do a job without pay. *All the basketball coaches are parent **volunteers**.* **vol·un·teers** *plural noun.* Plural of **volunteer**.

Ww

whisper   To speak in a very quiet voice. *I will **whisper** a secret to my friend.* **whis·per** *verb.*

wonderful   Very good. *My uncle cooked a **wonderful** dinner that my family enjoyed.* **won·der·ful** *adjective.*

wrinkled   Made a fold, ridge, or line in a smooth surface. *I **wrinkled** my shirt so much that my dad had to iron it.* **wrin·kled** *verb.* Past tense of **wrinkle**

483

Acknowledgments

The publisher gratefully acknowledges permission to reprint the following copyrighted materials:

"Abuelo and the Three Bears" by Jerry Tello, illustrations by Ana López Escrivá. Copyright © 1997 by Scholastic Inc. Reprinted with permission of Scholastic Inc.

"Babu's Song" by Stephanie Stuve-Bodeen, illustrated by Aaron Boyd. Text copyright © 2003 by Stephanie Stuve-Bodeen. Illustrations copyright © 2003 by Aaron Boyd. Reprinted by permission of Lee & Low Books, Inc.

"Bella Had a New Umbrella" by Eve Merriam from BLACKBERRY INK. Text copyright © 1985 by Eve Merriam. Reprinted with permission of William Morrow.

"Brush Dance" from POCKET POEMS by Robin Bernard. Text copyright © 2004 by Robin Bernard. Reprinted by permission of Penguin Putnam Books for Young Readers.

"Cat Kisses" by Bobbi Katz. Copyright © 1974 by Bobbi Katz. Reprinted with permission of the author.

"Click, Clack, Moo: Cows That Type" by Doreen Cronin, illustrated by Betsy Lewin. Text copyright © 2000 by Doreen Cronin. Illustrations copyright © 2000 by Betsy Lewin. Reprinted with permission from Simon & Schuster Books for Young Readers, an imprint of Simon & Schuster Children's Publishing Division.

"Crayons" from READ-ALOUD RHYMES FOR THE VERY YOUNG by Marchette Chute. Text copyright © 1974 by Marchette Chute. Reprinted by permission of Random House, Inc.

"Mr. Putter and Tabby Pour the Tea" by Cynthia Rylant, illustrated by Arthur Howard. Text copyright © 1994 by Cynthia Rylant. Illustrations copyright © 1994 by Arthur Howard. Reprinted with permission from Harcourt, Inc.

"My Name Is Yoon" by Helen Recorvits, illustrated by Gabi Swiatkowska. Text copyright © 2003 by Helen Recorvits. Illustrations copyright © 2003 by Gabi Swiatkowska. Reprinted with permission from Frances Foster Books, a division of Farrar, Straus and Giroux.

"One Grain of Rice: A Mathmatical Folktale" by Demi. Copyright © 1997 by Demi. Reprinted with permission of Scholastic Press, an imprint of Scholastic Inc.

"The Three Bears" from YOU READ TO ME, I'LL READ TO YOU: VERY SHORT FAIRY TALES TO READ TOGETHER by Mary Ann Hoberman, illustrated by Michael Emberley. Text copyright © 2004 by Mary Ann Hoberman. Illustrations copyright © 2004 by Michael Emberley. Used by permission of Little, Brown and Company.

"Doña Flor: A Tall Tale About A Giant Woman with a Big Heart" by Pat Mora, illustrated by Raul Colón. Text copyright © 2005 by Pat Mora. Illustrations copyright © 2005 by Raul Colón. Reprinted with permission of Random House, Inc.

"You'll Sing a Song and I'll Sing a Song" from THE ELLA JENKINS SONG BOOK FOR CHILDREN by Ella Jenkins. Text copyright © 1966 by Ella Jenkins. Reprinted with permission from Oak Publications (A Division of Embassy Music Corporation).

"You-Tú" from POCKET POEMS by Charlotte Pomerantz. Text copyright © 1960 by Charlotte Pomerantz. Reprinted with permission from Dutton Children's Books, a division of Penguin Young Readers Group.

ILLUSTRATIONS
Cover Illustration: Luciana Navarro Powell

10–27: Ed Martinez. 38–61: Arthur Howard. 62–63: Marisol Sarrazin. 64: Arthur Howard. 104: Daniel Del Valle. 110–111: Jason Wolff. 112–139: Gabi Swiatkowska. 146–147: Stacy Schuett. 148–149: Karen Dugan. 158–159: Rob Schuster. 160–189: Aaron Boyd. 198–199: Richard Torrey. 200–231: Raul Colon. 234: Daniel Del Valle. 250–251: Dominic Catalano. 252–279: Demi. 280–283: Valerie Sokolova. 290–311: Daniel Del Valle. 317: Anthony Lewis. 319: Doreen Gay-Kassel. 331: Kritina Rodanas. 352: Daniel Del Valle. 356–359: Jayoung Cho. 358–380: Ana Lopez Escriva. 382–385: Michael Emberly. 404–429: Betsy Lewin. 432: Peter Siu. 444: Beth G. Johnson. 462–463: Cecile Schoberle.

PHOTOGRAPHY
All photographs are by Ken Karp for Macmillan/McGraw-Hill (MMH) except as noted below.

iv: Blend Images/Alamy. v: (t) Siri Stafford/Getty Images; (c) George Ancona. vi: Joanna B. Pinneo/Aurora Photos. vii: Russell Kord/Alamy. viii: (tl) Richard Cummins/Corbis; (cl) Beatriz Schiller/Macmillan McGraw-Hill. ix: (tl) Pete Saloutos/Corbis; (bl bc) Courtesy Pam Munoz Ryan; (br) Steve Thanos Photography/Macmillan McGraw-Hill. 2-3: Blend Images/Alamy. 4–5: (bkgd) Wetzel & Company. 4: (b) Terry Vine/Patrick Lane/Getty Images. 5: (br) Notman/Library of Congress, LC-USZ62-13123. 6–7: Hutchings Stock Photography/digital light source. 8: (tr) Ariel Skelley/Corbis; (bl) Royalty-free/Corbis. 9: David Hanover/Stone/Getty Images. 11: Ed Martinez. 26: (tr) Cheron Bayna; (cl) Deborah Chabrian. 28: Sam Toren/Alamy. 29: Hans Georg Roth/Corbis. 30–31: (t) Imagebroker/Alamy. 30: (b) Blend Images/Alamy. 31: (t) Gary Conner/PhotoEdit. 32: Mike Powell/Getty Images. 33: Burke/Triolo/Brand X Pictures/Getty Images. 34–35: Ariel Skelley/Corbis. 36: (t) Burke/Triolo Productions/Brand X Pictures/Getty Images; (bl) Tim Ridley/DK Images; (bc) Erwin Bud Nielsen/Photolibrary. 37: Jim Cummins/Taxi/Getty Images. 60: Michael Papo. 64: Steve Cole/Getty Images. 65: Asia Images/Getty Images. 66–67: Siri Stafford/Getty Images. 68: (bkgd) Craig D. Wood/Panoramic Images; (t) Harald Sund/The Image Bank/Getty Images. 69: (t) Joseph Scherschel/Time Life Pictures/Getty Images; (b) Digital Vision/PunchStock. 70: North Wind Picture Archives. 71: Landing at Jamestown, 1607 (color litho), English School (17th century), Private Collection/The Bridgeman Art Library. 72: (tl) Dover Publications; (b) North Wind Picture Archives. 73: Keith Weller/USDA. 74: Panoramic Images/Getty Images. 76: Stockbyte/Getty Images. 77: (bkgd) Bet Noire/Shutterstock; (cr) PhotoLink/Getty Images; (bl) C Squared Studios/Getty Images. 78–79: Laura Dwight/Omni-Photo Communications. 80–81: (t) Digital vision/Getty Images. 80: (b) Richard T. Nowitz/Corbis. 81: (t) Digital vision/Getty Images; (cr) Myrleen Ferguson Cate/Photo Network/Alamy. 83–101: George Ancona. 102: Macmillan McGraw-Hill. 103: George Ancona. 106: Dennis MacDonald/PhotoEdit. 107: Tony Hutchings/Getty Images. 108–109: Ariel Skelley/Getty Images. 138: Courtesy Farrar, Strauss & Giroux. 140: (t) Dynamic Graphics/IT Stock Free/Alamy; (b) Brand X Pictures/PunchStock. 141: Jeff Greenberg/Alamy. 142: (b) Joe Hermosa/AP Images; (inset) Burke Triolo Productions/Getty Images. 143: Chris Rogers/Corbis. 144: David Young-Wolff/PhotoEdit. 145: Dave King/Dorling Kindersley/Getty Images. 152–153: Joanna B. Pinneo/Aurora Photos. 154–155: Digital Vision/PunchStock. 154: (b) Mitch Wojnarowicz/Amsterdam Recorder/The Image Works. 155: (br) Underwood & Underwood/Corbis. 156–157: Gabe Palmer/Corbis. 158: (bl) Photodisc/Getty Images; (bc) Ron Chapple/Thinkstock/Alamy. 159: Jeff Greenberg/PhotoEdit. 188: (t) Courtesy Stephanie Bodeen; (b) Courtesy Aaron Boyd. 190–193: (t b) PhotoDisc Green/Getty Images. 190: (bl) Tim Davis/Corbis. 191: (bkgd) Tim Davis/Corbis; (c) Photodisc Green/Getty Images. 192: (c) Jim Zucherman/Corbis. 193: (tr) Joe McDonald/Corbis. 194: Sean Justice/Corbis. 195: Marc Romanelli/Royalty Free/AGEfotostock. 196–197: Robert Michael/Corbis. 230 (t) Cheron Bayna; (b) Courtesy Raul Colon. 232–233: Dmitri Kessel/Time Life Pictures/Getty Images. 234: Juice Images/AGEfotostock. 235: David Buffington/Getty Images. 236–237: Russell Kord/Alamy. 238: VI/Alamy. 239: Comstock/PunchStock. 240: Robert Francis/Robert Harding Travel/Photolibrary. 241: Dave G. Houser/Corbis. 242–243: San Jacinto Museum of History. 244: Howie McCormick/AP Images. 246: Digital Vision. 247: (bkgd) Bet Noire/Shutterstock; (bl) C Squared Studios/Getty Images; (br) Ryan McVay/Getty Images; (cr) PhotoLink/Getty Images. 248–249: Jeff Greenberg/PhotoEdit. 278–279: Wetzel & Company. 278: (t) Courtesy Simon & Schuster. 284: Jade Albert Studio/Getty Images. 285: Dorling Kindersley/Getty Images. 286–287: The Granger Collection, New York. 288: (t) Photodisc Green/Getty Images; (bl) Courtesy George Greenwood. 289: Courtesy Sue Gregory. 290–311: (bkgd) Wetzel & Company. 292: (cl) Royalty Free/Corbis; (cr) Chris Collins/Corbis; (b) Ingram Publishing/Alamy. 293: (t) Image Farm; (b) Brown Brothers. 294: (c) Gibson Stock Photography. 295: (t) David Toase/Photodisc/Getty Images. 296: (c)

Jerry Schad/Photo Researchers; (cr) The Granger Collection, New York. 297: (c) The Granger Collection, New York. 298: (t) Image Farm; (b) Courtesy Newark Public Library. 299: (c) North Wind Picture Archives. 300: (c) Culver Pictures; (b) Courtesy The Newark Public Library. 301: (t) Corbis; (b) John Frank Nowikowski. 302: (t) Image Farm; (b) The Granger Collection, New York. 303: (c) George Washington Carver All -University Celebration,1998, Iowa State University. 304: (t cr) Bettmann/Corbis; (b) Brand X Pictures/Burke/Triolo Productions/Getty Images. 305: (t) Lars Klove/Getty Images; (c) Bettmann/Corbis. 306: (t) Image Farm; (b) Time Life Pictures/Getty Images. 307 308: (b) Courtesy Patricia E. Bath, M.D. 309: (t) Courtesy Patricia E. Bath, M.D. 310: (t) Image Farm; (tl) Courtesy Jim Haskins. 311: (t) David Toase/Photodisc/ Getty Images. 312: (t) Image Farm; (c) The Granger Collection, New York. 313: (tl) Courtesy George Greenwood; (tr) Image Farm. 314: Stockbyte/ Getty Images. 315: Michael Newman/PhotoEdit. 316–317: (t) Dorling Kindersley/Getty Images; (b) AsiaPix/Getty Images. 322–323: Richard Cummins/Corbis. 324: (b) Rubberball/AGEfotostock. 324–325: (l) Farinaz Taghavi/Getty Images; (2) Wetzel & Company. 325: (br) Pictorial Press Ltd/Alamy. 326-327: Bob Daemmrich/PhotoEdit. 328: (l) Comstock/ Getty Images; (b) Paul Slocombe/Next Century Images. 329: (t) Digital Vision Ltd./Getty Images; (b) Ingram Publishing/Alamy. 330–347: (bkgd) Beatriz Schiller/Macmillan McGraw-Hill. 348: Courtesy Sharon Dennis Wyeth. 349: Beatriz Schiller/Macmillan McGraw-Hill. 350-351: (bkgd) Wetzel & Company. 350: (b) BananaStock/Alamy. 351: (c) Photodisc Green/Getty Images. 352: Image 100/Royalty Free/Corbis. 353: Ed Zurga/ AP Images. 354-355: Dirk Anschutz/Getty Images. 380: Courtesy Jerry Tello. 386: Image DJ/Royalty Free/AGEfotostock. 387: Stockdisc/ PunchStock. 388–389: Pete Saloutos/Corbis. 390: (t) Richard T. Nowitz/ Corbis; (c) Michael Kooren/Reuters; (b) Richard T. Nowitz/Corbis. 391: Peter Charlesworth/On Asia; (br) Image Farm. 392: (t) Volker Steger/ Nordstar/Photo Researchers; (b) Jose Luis Pelaez, Inc./Corbis. 393: Institute of Cultural Relics and Archaeology of Henan Province/AP Images. 394: Vicky Alhadeff/Lebrecht Music and Arts Photo Library.

395: Toby Jacobs/Lebrecht Music and Arts Photo Library. 396: Ariane Kadoch/Dallas Morning News. 398: William Howard/Stone/Getty Images. 399: (cr) C Squared Studios/Getty Images; (l) Tracy Montana/ PhotoLink/Getty Images; (bkgd) Bet Noire/Shutterstock. 400–401: Masterfile. 428: Courtesy Simon and Schuster. 430–431: (bkgd) Arthur S. Aubry/Getty Images; (t) Library of Congress, LC-DIG-ppmsca-08795. 430: (b) North Wind Picture Archives. 434: MTPA Stock/Masterfile. 435: Rachel Epstein/PhotoEdit. 436–437: Tim Hall/Getty Images. 438: (bkgd) Wetzel & Company; (c) Susan Werner. 439: (bkgd) Wetzel & Company; (tr) Steve Thanos Photography/Macmillan McGraw-Hill. 440–441: (bkgd) Silver Editions 440: (t b) Courtesy Pam Munoz Ryan; (bl) Silver Editions. 441: (t b) Courtesy Pam Munoz Ryan. 442: (cl) Silver Editions; (cr) Courtesy Pam Munoz Ryan. 443: (bl) Silver Editions; (bc) Courtesy Pam Munoz Ryan. 444, 445, 446: Courtesy Pam Munoz Ryan. 446: (br) Silver Editions. 447: (tl) Stock Montage/SuperStock; (tr) Bettmann/Corbis; (c) Macmillan McGraw-Hill. 448: Courtesy Pam Munoz Ryan. 449: (t cl) Silver Editions; (c) Courtesy Pam Munoz Ryan. 450 through 455: Steve Thanos Photography/Macmillan McGraw-Hill. 451: (br) Silver Editions. 453: (tr bl) Silver Editions. 454: (br) Silver Editions. 455: (tl) Silver Editions; (b) Courtesy Pam Munoz Ryan. 456, 457: Courtesy Pam Munoz Ryan. 460: Richard Hutchings/Photo Researchers. 461: Tom Stewart/Corbis. 464: Joe Atlas/Royalty Free/ AGEfotostock. 465: Digital Vision/Getty Images. 468: (l) J. David Andrews/Masterfile; (r) Lori Adamski Peek/Getty Images. 469: (t) Ariel Skelley/Masterfile; (b) U.S. Fish & Wildlife Service/Dick Bailey. 470: Joeseph Sohm-Visions of America/Getty Images. 471: Ariel Skelley. 472: Nigel Cattlin/Photo Researchers. 473: (t) Corbis; (b) W Productions/ Getty Images. 474: Steve Allen/Brand X Pictures/AGEfotostock. 475: Taxi/ Getty Images. 476: Dick Bailey/U.S. Fish & Wildlife Service. 477: Photo Spin/Getty Images. 478: Brand X Pictures/PunchStock. 479: Royalty-Free/ Corbis. 480: Lori Adamski Peek/Getty Images. 481: Davis Barber/ PhotoEdit. 483: (c) David Young-Wolff/PhotoEdit; (b) Ken Cavanagh/ Macmillan McGraw-Hill.

Decoding Strategy Chart

Step 1	Look for word parts (prefixes) at the beginning of the word.
Step 2	Look for word parts (suffixes) at the end of the word.
Step 3	In the base word, look for familiar spelling patterns. Think about the six syllable-spelling patterns you have learned.
Step 4	Sound out and blend together the word parts.
Step 5	Say the word parts fast. Adjust your pronunciation as needed. Ask yourself: "Is this a word I have heard before?" Then read the word in the sentence and ask: "Does it make sense in this sentence?"